MW01228739

First Yes, Then I Do

A WEDDING PLANNER & MEMOIR

From Intimate To Extravagant: A wedding memoir and wedding planner with tips & tricks plus insider secrets that will make your special day spectacular!

A Special Thank You

We would like to give a special thank you to all of the countless numbers of vendors and couples who have shared their experiences, tips & tricks as well as their ultimate wedding planning secrets with us. Of course we can't forget our parents and family members who helped us and took on key roles in our own wedding. As you will see, many of the stories you will read come from that experience. This wedding planner and memoir is dedicated to our three daughters whom we love with all of our hearts. In large part, this wedding planner and memoir was created for them.

Contact Us

We would like to hear from you about how this book helped you in your wedding journey. Email us at firstyesthenido@infinancer.com and tell us your story. Your story may be featured in future editions and/or writings!

For bulk purchases please submit your inquiry to firstyesthenido@infinancer.com with the term "Bulk Purchase Inquiry" in the subject line.

If you would like to contact Lucy and Adam for speaking opportunities you can do so via email at adam@infinancer.com with the term "Speaking Inquiry" in the subject line.

Legal Disclaimer And Terms Of Use

The authors and publisher of this book and the accompanying materials have used their best efforts in preparing this book. The authors and publisher make no representation or warranties with respect to the accuracy, applicability, fitness or completeness of the contents of this publication. The information contained in this book is strictly for educational purposes. Therefore, if you wish to apply ideas contained in this book, you are taking full responsibility for your actions. Neither the publisher nor author shall be held liable or responsible for any loss or damage allegedly arising from any suggestion or information contained in this book.

Copyright 2023 © InFinancer - All Rights Reserved

Table Of Contents

Introduction

Introduction

First of all, we want to congratulate you on getting engaged! This is such an exciting time for you and your sweetheart and you probably have a million things swirling in your head about what the wedding is going to be like and where to start first. Well, the first place to start is to enjoy being engaged. Enjoy the moment! After you take it all in, then start the planning phase.

This book will help you write the very first chapter of your own story of marriage. We encourage you to not only take notes everywhere in the book and in the "My Thoughts" section, but use it as a journal to write your experiences, thoughts and emotions down. This book is meant to be saved, cherished and even passed down as a testament to the beginning of your legacy as a married couple.

You might ask why should you choose this wedding planner over thousands of others? There are definitely some that are more pretty. There are definitely some that have their own formula of what to do and when to do it. There definitely are some that have been created by people who have been in the wedding scene longer than us or have a bigger name. What we think sets this apart is the number of professionals we have had conversations with, the number of engaged couples we have encountered and the amount of information we have gathered and narrowed down so that you can make the best choices for your own wedding. It's not your traditional wedding planner.

We want you to be placed in a position, in terms of knowledge and preparation, to where you can maximize whatever budget you have and focus on what is most important to you. Oh, and we like to have fun along the way so hopefully you'll get some laughs out of it too!

So where did this all begin? For Lucy, it started when she was playing wedding princess as a little girl. For me, it started when I began working in the Engagement & Wedding Jewelry Industry. That is actually where Lucy and I first met. We were working for the same company. Years down the line I ended up proposing to her and, as you could imagine, she was an expert on jewelry, diamonds & proposals as well, so there was no way I could cruise by with the old solitaire and propose at dinner routine.

I had to find a way to uncover what her idea of the perfect ring was and she knew all the tricks. I had to get a lovely diamond and she knew all about diamonds. I had to set up the proposal and she knew all the tricks and heard all of the proposal ideas from the clients we were in front of. Essentially, my romance game had to be at an elite level to pull it off and I think I did.

Although Lucy didn't spend 20 years in the engagement and wedding jewelry industry as I did, she did spend most of her time with future brides & grooms while we were working together and then continued these conversations as she moved into the beauty industry. It gives us a unique perspective because we both were so curious and inquisitive about how couples went about planning their wedding from their point of view as well as the knowledge of the hundreds of wedding experts we worked with and had relationships with along the way.

This allowed us to come up with what we feel is the most comprehensive list of tips, insider secrets, real world scenarios and planner worksheets that has been put together.

Pretty good reason to choose First Yes, Then I Do, right? Well, there's a bit more to our story!

Adam won't tell you this because of his humble nature, but he is an amazing coach. A life-changing coach as many of his clients have attested to. He's worked with individuals and businesses on financial habits, self improvement habits, accountability, personal growth and so much more. Where he really shines in this book is through the perspective of a financial coach and personal coach. Adding small things here and there that can change your mindset on where to spend money and why. He makes the simplest statement or asks a certain question that allows you to gain some self-insight into what is most important to you and your sweetheart during this spectacular time in your life.

Now to the WHY!

Adam's Why: To curb marriage issues & divorce due to money issues. I can make an impact by coaching people to have fewer money issues and more money communication. Believe it or not, it starts before the wedding. It starts the moment you get engaged. Money communication is key. Money & the stress around it is one of the biggest reasons marriages fail. If I can reach even just a few people and open the communication and mindset, it would mean less divorces which leads to less collateral damage (the children). Intact families create the most productive members of society because there is less anxiety and more complete & impactful role models available for children at home. The studies showing this don't lie. So this means I can change the world, right? SO CAN YOU!!!

Lucy's Why: I totally agree with Adam and love his Why for the pre-marriage and early marriage aspect of his wonderfully powerful coaching. Having been in the beauty industry for quite some time now, I also have the perspective of the brides who want to be as close as possible to their dream wedding. We all know we can't get married in a castle to a prince, but we sure can get the same feeling as a princess by creating a special moment in time in our own, individualistic way. Plus, as someone who has done hair and now focuses on eyelash beauty, beautification can definitely help you look like the princess you are when you are about to walk down the aisle to say "I do". I want every woman to have their princess moment!

Other services we offer:

Everything Proposals

- Diamond & jewelry tutorials
- How to propose from finding her style to gaining leverage & saving at the jewelry store
- Videos, group coaching & one on one coaching

Scan To Learn More

Jewelry Education

- How to recognize quality in jewelry before you buy
- Diamond education
- Precious metals & how they will wear
- Important insider secrets that will help you save money

Scan To Learn More

Everything Weddings

- Ultimate Wedding Planner Secret Sheets (Excel or Google Sheets)
- Digital, soft, hard or bulk copies of First Yes, Then I Do
- Free Bonus Gifts for purchasing this book

Scan To Learn More

Budget Coaching

Scan To Learn More

- Learn how to budget with consistent or inconsistent income
- Discover habits that will create your legacy
- Create a path out of debt & harness the full potential of your income

Bootcamps

Scan To Learn More

- Intense & focused sessions that achieve results quickly
- Marriage & Money Bootcamps for couples, Startup Bootcamps for aspiring coaches & more.
- Video, Group & 1 on 1

Group Challenges

Scan To Learn More

- Connect with people who have the same goals
- Commit to improving yourself
- Change in ways you never have been able to do before on your own

Master Lash Artist

- Classic, hybrid, volume & mega volume eyelash extensions
- Lash lifts
- Lash & brow tinting
- Special events or just because
- Experience a luxurious lash transformation

Scan To Learn More

One On One Coaching

InFinancer

- Find your why, the driving factor behind taking action
- Meaningful & powerful sessions designed for you
- Focus on habits, mindset & accountability

Scan To Learn More

Legacy Story Podcast

- Stories that will inspire you to create your own legacy
- Lessons passed on from one on one coaching sessions
- Fun & mind-grabbing episodes to help you gain self insight

Scan To Learn More

First Things First

First Things First

Celebrate your relationship! Take some time to think back on how you met, the great times you have had, the defining moments. Write down how the proposal happened and the thoughts the both of you had right before and right after you said yes. As you begin to envision your wedding day, keep these moments in mind. Most importantly, keep how much you love each other in mind throughout the wedding planning process. Less stress, more love.

In this book, you are going to find sections for each major area in a wedding budget. These sections are Questions To Ask, Tips & Tricks, Things You May Not Have Thought About & Insider Secrets. You'll also find planning sheets to fill out, a to-do list that you can fill out for most sections and a place to write notes that pop into your head or experiences that you have along the way.

This book also serves as a timeless memoir that you can look back on, read and reminisce on this defining moment in your life. Just like the love note on the back of the book states, the beginning of your story may be different from the middle of it, but the one thing that will endure is the love that you have for each other.

The beginning of our story will be different from the middle, that is for sure. In the end, our love will be our greatest legacy. I love you! XOXOXO

How We Met

Favorite Memories

The Proposal

Our Wedding Vision

_____

_____

_____

_____

_____

_____

_____

_____

_____

_____

_____

_____

_____

_____

_____

_____

_____

_____

_____

_____

_____

_____

_____

My Vows

My Sweetheart's Vows

Thank You Speech

Important Dates

Date Of Engagement	Engagement Party	Bridal Shower	Bachelorette Party	Bachelor Party

Final Dress Fitting	Rehearsal Date/Time	Wedding Date	Honeymoon Departure	Honeymoon Return

Now for some very important tips before we begin with each facet of the wedding.

Make sure that the marriage is the priority and not the wedding itself. You may disagree on some things for the wedding. You may disagree on a lot for the wedding. When all is said and done, the most important thing is the relationship and the marriage.

Everything doesn't have to be decided right away. One of the biggest mistakes is to hammer your partner with dozens and dozens of thoughts on the wedding in a single day (after you have celebrated the engagement of course).

Remember, it's the groom's day too. The groom can have great ideas and if we can tell you one thing it is this; the ideas they do have are usually coming from a more sentimental place and are more connected to him than the latest Pinterest craze.

Think timeless, not trendy.

Everyone knows how to research for top rated vendors, but the total stars you see shouldn't determine who you choose. The latest stars do! Always go into the comment section and change the filter option to newest. This allows you see how they are TODAY, not 6 years ago when they had different management and a completely different team. There could be some major changes in how they do business and that 4.5 stars that looks good overall has nothing to do with the 1 to 3 star reviews they have been getting the last 6 months. Your vendor could have suddenly become sour with their job and not like it anymore. Maybe they changed management or staff and their recent work has been sub-par. Would you still want them?

When you book the vendor of your dreams, potentially one of the vendors from your priority list, ask them if they have preferred vendors that they would recommend. They know their work, recommend them knowing their reputation is at stake for doing so and have worked with them in the past which might actually make your wedding day run smoother.

Trust your intuition when making informed decisions. You don't want to get caught up in what others have done, what your family wants you to do or what you think they want you to do. Your intuition comes from a place of what YOU want to do as a couple. You know, the most important people in the equation.

Find wedding vendors that get your priorities, your vision as well as your goals for the wedding.

Meet your vendors in person. It's all about the vibe.

Don't assume anything. Read every word of every contract! If you don't, you may sign a contract with the entertainment that requires their transportation to be covered among other things. Set up & break down as well as cleaning fees might be on your vendor contract outside of the fees given to you for the venue itself. You may have already signed a non-refundable contract with a wedding planner and then the next thing you know, your reception site requires you to use theirs . . . and they aren't cheap. Now you're paying for 2 planners and only using one. When we say every word of every contract, we mean it!

Things to ask EVERY vendor:

1. Are you available for my date?
2. What is included with your services?
3. What are the costs of your services?
4. Can you work within our budget?
5. How long have you been doing this?
6. Can I see recent photographs/videos of weddings you have done?
7. How many weddings do you book on a weekend?
8. Will you book other weddings on my wedding day?
9. Have you worked at venues similar to ours?
10. How much time do you need to set up and break down?
11. What are the overtime fees?
12. Do you have licenses & insurance?
13. How much is the deposit and when is the final payment due?
14. Do you have a contract we can read before making a decision?
15. What additional fees should we expect?
16. Will you personally be working with us or will someone else be assigned?
17. What are the contingency plans if for some reason you cannot provide services the day of the wedding?
18. What is the cancellation policy?

Guests

Guests

Let's be honest. Planning a wedding will more than likely be stressful. Stressful to you and stressful for your fiance. The first areas that you will be focusing on is how many people you are going to invite, who you are going to invite and your budget. Adam & I had quite a few disagreements when we were planning our wedding. Most couples we have had conversations with admitted to getting into spats while planning. The countless number of wedding vendors we spoke with readily gave up big fight horror stories. It happens. It's normal. We decided to have a safe word that would let the other person know they were overwhelmed, agitated or needed a timeout from planning. We even used it on the wedding day. The code word? SPATULA!

What To Ask Yourselves

- Who do we absolutely have to have at our wedding?
- Who are people we would like to have at our wedding?
- Who do we feel obligated to invite to our wedding?
- Who has invited us to their wedding in the last 12 months?
- How many people are we going to allow each of our parents to invite?
- Do we want children at the wedding?
- Do we limit plus ones? If so, is the plus one limited to people we know or serious relationships only?

Things You Haven't Thought About

- If a family member is contributing to your wedding fund, you may have more than 2 decision makers when it comes to the guest list.
- Have you thought about removing the plus one? You may want to consider it before you realize you don't recognize a third of the people in

your wedding album.

- Consider an adults only wedding.
- Think about reception-only invites. If your ceremony is in a different place it may save on additional rentals. This would be the opposite of a ceremony only invite, which is highly frowned upon etiquette-wise.
- Does your significant other have family or cultural traditions that require certain people to be invited, even if you don't know them? It is important to have this conversation and also see if you can set certain boundaries without completely ditching the tradition.
- If you're thinking about adding your neighbors to the guest list, re-think it. Unless you hang out and BBQ together, play board games on Thursday nights and are the godparent to one of their kids.
- You know that one friend or family member that "gets lit" at every gathering. Think twice before adding them to the list.

Tips & Tricks

- Keep in mind that your first brainstorm list isn't the final list. There may be people you take off the list and there may be people that completely slipped your mind. Sorry Aunt Gertrude!
- Set firm boundaries with other decision makers on who they can invite. No Mom, your friend from hot yoga class that you talk to for 30 minutes twice a month doesn't qualify for a spot on the guest list.
- Start with your must-have guests. Typically this is family and very close friends. This list will also serve as your "emergency list" aka the pandemic list just in case you have to severely limit the number of people who can attend.
- If you don't have a real relationship with a coworker outside of the confines of business, it's safe to not invite them.
- You are not obligated to invite Jessie & Skip whose wedding you attended in 2014, even though it was off the hook. I mean, you haven't talked to them in four years.
- Create a tiered list with your VIPs in list A. Relatives you don't speak to that much, friends that you only spend time with occasionally and co-workers you have a personal relationship with in tier B. List C may be people you are on the fence about. List D will be people you are only inviting out of degrees of separation, respect or if you feel guilty by not inviting them. Send out invites via batches in that order. Once you receive some declined invitations you will be able to add to the next group.

- If there is a group of people that you wanted to invite but you simply couldn't invite them due to budget or maximum occupancy, throw a second reception. Except this one would probably be at a house and be more casual.
- Many wedding experts out there say ditch the kids, or at least the young ones for the wedding. We have to push back on this a little bit. If cousin Shelton who you are close with has 4 kids with his wife and will be traveling from Florida to Arizona for the wedding, how is that going to work out? Are they leaving the kids in Florida? What if they are young? What if they don't know anyone to leave them with in Arizona? What if you set an age limit as is often suggested and the opt-in invite age is 12 years old but your best friend Solandra is coming to San Juan Capistrano from Morro Bay and has a 13 and a 7 year old? It's OK to make exceptions but if it isn't obvious to the other guests (who left kids behind) you may have a bit of backlash headed your way.

Insider Secrets

- Create a rule among your family members, especially both sets of parents, for guest list additions to only include people you have actually met. Most of the time you won't get pushback on this one.
- Once your list is created, revisit the list and highlight anyone that you haven't spent time with in the last 12 months. Circle the highlighted name if you don't plan on seeing them in the next 6 months. If they are circled and highlighted, maybe they don't need an invite. If they are highlighted, keep them on the list and know that if push comes to shove, they will be one of the first ones off for budget's sake.
- Get your guest list mostly solidified before you go looking for venues.
- Use the phone number rule. If you don't have their phone number in either of your contacts, then they probably shouldn't be invited. This also helps when you have to make a follow up call if they haven't RSVPd.
- Pick your bridesmaids carefully. Your bridesmaids are there to make your day as easy as possible for you. They are there to help. If Felicia is known for not wanting to do anything and only shows up to parties or dinners but never helps . . . . say bye Felicia! At least to your bridesmaid troupe.

Guests - To Do List

- [ ] _____
- [ ] _____
- [ ] _____
- [ ] _____
- [ ] _____
- [ ] _____
- [ ] _____
- [ ] _____
- [ ] _____
- [ ] _____
- [ ] _____
- [ ] _____
- [ ] _____
- [ ] _____
- [ ] _____
- [ ] _____
- [ ] _____
- [ ] _____
- [ ] _____

My Thoughts

First Name	Last Name	Address	Sent Save The Date	Sent Invitation	Number Of Guests Wedding	Attending Wedding	Children	Number Of Guests Rehearsal	Attending Rehearsal	Table	Out Of Town Guest

First Name	Last Name	Address	Sent Save The Date	Sent Invitation	Number Of Guests Wedding	Attending Wedding	Children	Number Of Guests Rehearsal	Attending Rehearsal	Table	Out Of Town Guest

First Name	Last Name	Address	Sent Save The Date	Sent Invitation	Number Of Guests Wedding	Attending Wedding	Children	Number Of Guests Rehearsal	Attending Rehearsal	Table	Out Of Town Guest

First Name	Last Name	Address	Sent Save The Date	Sent Invitation	Number Of Guests Wedding	Attending Wedding	Children	Number Of Guests Rehearsal	Attending Rehearsal	Table	Out Of Town Guest

First Name	Last Name	Address	Sent Save The Date	Sent Invitation	Number Of Guests Wedding	Attending Wedding	Children	Number Of Guests Rehearsal	Attending Rehearsal	Table	Out Of Town Guest

Budget

Budget

I'm the budget guy. I love helping couples navigate a pretty difficult topic that needs to be discussed for wedding planning and for life together after "I Do" as well. This can be a difficult conversation to have especially if you alone or your sweetheart don't really budget in the first place. Now you are talking about working together on a budget. Yikes! Neither of you should be too overbearing. I can picture Lucy's eyes rolling right now just at the mere mention of the budget. After she realized my why when it comes to focusing on the budget the discussions became much easier. Lucy is still cute even with the eye roll though, so there's that.

What To Ask Yourself

- How much money do we have saved outside of an emergency fund?
- How much money can we realistically put into a sinking fund each month?
- Who else might be contributing to the wedding fund?
- Are we willing to start our marriage off with debt and if so, how much vs what we pay in cash?
- Are we going to feel less joy on our special day by spending less and not going overboard?
- Are we going full on DIY or full on wedding planner? Perhaps a combination of the two?
- Do we want the courthouse wedding, the backyard wedding, the public park/beach wedding, the rented house wedding, the traditional venue wedding, the destination wedding or the elegant all-out ballroom wedding?

Things You Haven't Thought About

- The Average Wedding Cost is $28k.
- 44% of couples say figuring out and managing their wedding budget is the most challenging part of planning their wedding.
- 66% of couples go over budget for their wedding.
- When breaking down your per person budget don't forget service charges (15-25%) and tax before you do it. Once you add this you will have the actual per guest cost.
- Did you know negotiation is a thing? Really, it is! Try negotiating with your vendors, especially if you can pay in cash!!!
- Get a side gig. Imagine if you and your sweetheart put in an extra 10 hours a week each with a side gig. Pretty big dent in your cash on hand for the wedding right?
- Evaluate your WANTS versus your NEEDS in order to cut costs.

Tips & Tricks

- Budget first. All things should come from this budget. This may mean you might have to cut down on the guest list to reach the budget you set.
- If you haven't already made it a habit to budget, you might want to make a budget for each of you individually before you dive into the budget for the wedding. Knowing where your own money is going is paramount. It also makes it easier to do it as a couple for the wedding and once the two of you are married.
- Make a commitment to stay as close as possible to your ideal budget.
- Itemize everything. Find a wedding spreadsheet that calculates costs for you and is detailed. We know of one because we created it, it's AWESOME & it covers virtually every section in this book! You can find it at https://www.infinancer.com/weddings
- Small things can add up quickly. Pinterest is going to challenge your budget because you will see all of these great ideas and if you keep adding and adding . . . you are also adding to your overall costs.
- If you find that you are saving less than what you planned each month for the wedding or that you are spending more than you planned, you need to address the issue immediately. Don't bury your head in the sand before you end up burying yourself in debt to start off the marriage.
- Research vendors and where the wedding is going to be before creating your final budget. Set a time limit though (15 minutes per potential

vendor). You don't want your research to be a rabbit-hole-inducing time monster. Quick research to gather cost estimates. That's it.

♥ Let's play a game. You've budgeted for a wedding that is going to cost $40,000. The average age of a couple getting married is 30. If you were to shave $10,000 off of the wedding budget and place it into a wedding day mutual fund with an average gain of 10% . . . that 10k will be over $100K when you turn 55. That would be a great Silver Year (25th) Anniversary gift wouldn't it?

♥ What is the old saying? If you don't ask, you don't get. Ask for discounts. Ask for free add-ons. Ask, ask, ask!

♥ Do you go to church? Many churches have women's organizations or clubs that would be happy to help with your DIY or prep for a small donation.

♥ See if you can receive a discount for posting an honest positive review on a vendor's YELP, Google, Facebook Page, etc.

♥ You'll be surprised how much you can save by editing your guest list and removing the 20 people you were on the fence about in the first place.

♥ Choose a month or day that isn't typical for weddings. You'll save money.

♥ Choose a time that isn't typical. Instead of serving a full meal, perhaps your 2PM wedding reception will have hors d'oeuvres as the signature fare.

♥ Instead of having the wedding in 10 months, extend the timeframe so that you can save more.

♥ Getting money from the parents or a relative? Remember this often means they are going to want to have some input on the who/what/when/where of the wedding. It's OK to talk to them before the planning starts to set boundaries of where you would like input.

♥ If there is no way around using a credit card, and you know you can pay it off within a short period of time, at least have the purchases work for you by way of airline mileage for the honeymoon.

♥ Don't forget to budget gratuity for your vendors. Yes, most of them expect it.

♥ Can you get a 2 for 1 with one or more of your vendors? An example would be a DJ that also has lighting for the entire reception area.

♥ Your budget is going to be anchored directly to the number of guests that you are inviting.

♥ If you are putting something on a credit card, ask yourself if you can pay it off in 30 days. If not, reconsider your budget and your ability to pay for the wedding of your dreams. It can still be dreamy on a budget . . . but your credit card bills can become a nightmare.

- Self care is paramount when dealing with the stresses of planning a wedding. Budget for it. The reason I suggest self care as part of your budget is because it is essential to take days off from wedding planning or even talking about the wedding or ceremony. Have a date night where discussing the wedding is off limits. A couples massage. Something, anything, just for the two of you.
- Have a wedding Budget Date night.
- Have a Guest List Date Night.
- Think about not having bridesmaids & groomsmen. Instead, invite the people who would have filled those spots for a special toast (champagne, mimosas or bourbon) to start your wedding day.
- The biggest way to save money is to elope. Find a super beautiful place for you, your sweetheart, the officiant and the photographer/videographer and livestream the ceremony. On your 1 year anniversary, throw a huge party and invite the people you would have invited to the wedding. You don't have to have the party as formal as expected on the day of the wedding . . . but you still can if you want.
- Downsize your bridal party to cut costs.
- No, your co-workers do not need to be invited.
- Have any friends that have been married recently? If you remember what their decorations looked like and think they still have them, maybe they will let you borrow them. They may just give them to you.
- Don't forget to compare buying new, buying used and renting.
- Sign up for junk mail with vendors you would consider using or places that sell the things you need for the wedding. You never know when that major sale or deal pops up that you can grab.
- Do it yourself whenever possible, start early and make sure it's on the right things. You don't want to spend two months creating DIY party favors only to see half of them left on the table after the wedding.
- Ask friends or family to exchange their skills in lieu of a gift or at a deep discount for the wedding. Do you know a musician, DJ, baker, chef, aspiring photographer, videographer, etc?

Insider Secrets

- Keep Personal Finances & Financial Goals at the forefront when creating your budget.
- You will have an "ideal" estimated budget which will eventually morph into a more realistic budget which will then morph into the actual budget.
- Make a Top 3 List. Each of you, individually. The top 3 things, in order

of importance, that you are willing to spend the most on. Make it a game. Don't tell each other. Just write it down. Then reveal it to one another. Discuss the list. Be mindful of the reason it is important to your sweetie. Then consolidate it into a top 3 list that both of you agree on.

- Book your priority vendors first.
- Take into consideration family and/or cultural traditions when finalizing your budget.
- Remember, there are things that we are talking about in this book that will last a lifetime such as your wedding rings, the pictures and/or the video. On the flip side there are things that are really for other people and are only for that day. Flowers, Food and Entertainment. Your budget may want to lean more on the forever things and less on the others. Very few people are going to remember the food they were served in 6 months let alone a year later.
- The knock it out of the park money saving day: Get your hair trial and makeup trial done and then go have your engagement photos done right before your engagement party. You'll be all done up, capture some great photos and can have the photographer stick around for capturing the party as well.
- Go to a bridal show. Not to necessarily book vendors but to do some research. Ask each vendor that you stop to talk to what the #1 question people should ask, but don't. They'll all have different questions that they think should be asked, but it will give you great insight into what is currently on the minds of those vendors. After all, we don't update this book every month!
- Remember the Top 3 priorities game? Try out the lowest 3 priorities as well. This may help you spend less money on the least important aspects of the wedding.
- Choose items you can re-sell or re-use. We re-used our centerpiece vases for decor around our house. Some have shells and sand in them. Some have rocks from our travels. Some have . . . you know . . . flowers. The motif candle boxes aren't all used almost 10 years later but come in handy for parties, bubble baths and blackouts.
- Don't make a purchase or book a vendor within 24 hours. Wait one full day to fully understand and process what the cost means for your budget. If you still think it is the right move after 24 hours or more, go for it.
- Just like with your personal budget, if you run over in one area, you are going to have to be flexible enough to cut in another area. Remember the high and low priority game? Take from the low priorities if you go over budget in the high priorities.

Budget - To Do List

- [ ] _____
- [ ] _____
- [ ] _____
- [ ] _____
- [ ] _____
- [ ] _____
- [ ] _____
- [ ] _____
- [ ] _____
- [ ] _____
- [ ] _____
- [ ] _____
- [ ] _____
- [ ] _____
- [ ] _____
- [ ] _____
- [ ] _____
- [ ] _____
- [ ] _____

My Thoughts

Apparel/Beautification	Estimated	Actual
Gown		
Bridal Shoes		
Hair		
Makeup		
Eyelashes		
Jewelry		
Manicure/Pedicure		
Honeymoon Lengerie		
Bridesmaid Dresses		
Bridesmaid Accessories		
Bridesmaid Shoes		
Groom's Tux/Suit		
Groom's Shoes		
Groom's Accessories		
Groomsmen Tuxes/Suits		
Alterations		
Eng. Party/Rehearsal Dinner Fits		
Gown Preservation		
Garters		
Total Apparel		

Parties	Estimated	Actual
Catering		
Bartender		
Liquor		
Tables/Chairs		
Decorations		
Gifts		
Music		
Flowers		
Day Trips (Bach. Party)		
Hotels		
Airfare		
Gratuity		
Food		
Entertainment		
Total		

Stationery

Stationery	Estimated	Actual
Save The Date		
Invitations		
Direction Cards		
RSVP Cards		
Postage		
Calligrapher		
Hotel Welcome Package Notes		
Ceremony Welcome Board		
Reception Welcome Board		
Table Cards		
Bar Signage		
Menu Cards		
Bachelor/ette Party Invitations		
Wedding Programs		
Thank You Notes		
Total Stationery		

Jewelry

Jewelry	Estimated	Actual
Wedding bands		
Sizings, Egravings, Modifications		
Accessories		
Total Rings		

Photography/Videography

Photography/Videography	Estimated	Actual
Engagement Shoot		
Reception		
Ceremony		
Photo albums		
Video Editing/Video Production		
Total Photography		

Ceremony	Estimated	Actual
Clergy		
Location fee		
Altar decorations		
Chair Rentals		
Chair Covers		
Guest Book		
Ring Bearer Pillow		
Flower Girl Basket		
Unity Candle		
Aisle Runner		
Ushers		
Gratuity		
Transportation		
Childcare		
Total Ceremony		

Flowers	Estimated	Actual
Wedding Bouquet		
Bridesmaid Bouquets		
Corsages		
Boutonnières		
Reception Centerpieces		
Ceremony Placements		
Aisle Floral Pieces		
Throw Away Bouquet		
Rose Petals/Flower Girl Flowers		
Total Flowers		

Gifts	Estimated	Actual
Attendant gifts		
Gift for fiancee		
Favors		
Total Gifts & Favors		

Reception

Reception	Estimated	Actual
Venue		
Caterer		
Cake		
Desserts		
Musician		
Bartender		
Liquor		
Security		
Groom's Cake		
Cake Knife		
Cake Decorations		
Cake Table/Display		
Servers		
Table Decorations		
Other Decorations		
Dishes		
Glassware		
Napkins		
Linens		
Tables		
Chairs		
Lighting		
Entertainment		
Rice/Rose petals/Bubbles		
Parking		
Gratuities		
Limousine		
Guest Transportation		
Childcare		
Misc.		
Total Reception		

Honeymoon

Honeymoon	Estimated	Actual
Airfare		
Accommodations		
Transportation		
Entertainment		
Cash		
Total Honeymoon		

Other Expenses

Other Expenses	Estimated	Actual
Marriage License		
Wedding Planner		
Day Of Coordinator		
Hotel Block Deposit		
Additional Reception Dress		
Additional Reception Shoes		
Other		
Other		
Other		
Other		
Other		
Total Misc		

	Estimated	Actual
Grand Total		

Wedding Rings
&
Jewelry

Wedding Rings & Jewelry

Let's talk about the shiny stuff! Adam & I worked in the engagement ring, diamond and wedding band industry and for the same company. I was schooled on metals, diamonds and quality but not to the extent that Mr. Diamontologist over here was. I also spent a lot of time talking to couples about their engagement and wedding. Basically, Adam knew he couldn't just do the ordinary thing and he absolutely did not do ordinary! He tricked me using friends to get the style that I loved. He had my old coworkers sneakily get my ring size. Adam bought me a new lens for my SLR camera after we moved to L.A. and suggested we go to San Diego to take photos of our favorite places for a collage. Little did I know he was documenting our engagement day and I was totally surprised when he asked me to marry him. He had friends and family meet up with us afterwards and after all of that, when I went to bed to go to sleep that night, there was a lighted box on my pillow that had my favorite color gemstone placed in a right hand ring. I think he did alright, don't you?

What To Ask A Jeweler

- Do you have a jeweler onsite?
- What type of warranties do you have?
- What sets you apart from competitors?
- Do you have wedding rings within my price range?

- ♥ Do you offer free polishing and cleanings or is there an added cost for that?
- ♥ Do you have any maintenance packages that go with the ring or can be purchased?
- ♥ Is the first time sizing free?
- ♥ How long would it take to size a ring?
- ♥ How long would it take to special order a ring?
- ♥ Can I customize a ring?
- ♥ What is the process for a custom ring?
- ♥ Do you carry other jewelry like earrings, pendants and pearls?

Things You Haven't Thought About

- ♥ Special Order Time Frame
- ♥ Sizing fees
- ♥ Diamond Warranties
- ♥ Cleaning & Polishing
- ♥ Insurance
- ♥ Engraving
- ♥ Ring Boxes
- ♥ Wedding Day Jewelry such as pearls and earrings.

Tips & Tricks

- ♥ Gone are the days of 3 piece wedding ring sets that come with the engagement ring and two wedding bands. That's actually a good thing because everyone has their own style. This also means you probably need to get your wedding rings still.
- ♥ I have created a more in depth course on how to recognize quality jewelry including engagement rings, wedding bands and diamonds. You can find it at https://www.infinancer.com/jewelry
- ♥ A jeweler onsite means that your sizings, cleaning, polishing & engraving will be done quicker. Imagine having your rings shipped out to a different location every time you need something done. Now imagine if the rings were shipped out and came back with deep scratches or incomplete work. That's right, they have to be sent out again.
- ♥ My Master Jeweler used to always say… good work is never cheap and cheap work is never good.
- ♥ Your rings need to be sturdy and able to handle wear and tear. Super thin

rings, even in precious metals will not last forever and will more than likely bend out of shape often. Make sure they are not hollowed out or thinner than 2mm.

- Look out for porosity! Ask to see the ring under a gemscope or microscope and look for what seems to be little pits or bumps in the ring. This is a sign of poor craftsmanship or inadequate quality control.

- If you are looking for rings with diamonds, make sure that all of the stones are matching in color and clarity. You don't want one diamond darker than another. It will be that more noticeable when dirty.

- Eternity bands, Tungsten, Titanium, Ceramic Carbide and many other non-precious metals will most likely need to be special ordered in your size. Expect a 6-8 week delivery time and give yourself TWICE that just in case it comes in completely wrong and they have to order it all over again.

- Most of the top jewelers have a diamond warranty that covers chipping, cracking and/or loss of a diamond as long as you have it inspected once or twice a year to keep the warranty valid. They'll usually clean and polish your ring during the inspection and it will look like the day you were married when you get it back.

- First time sizing for free is pretty standard in the jewelry industry.

- Some jewelers will have additional maintenance packages as an add on where you can pay one fee and have as many cleanings, polishings & sizings done as you'd like for a certain amount of time or for life. If the cost is equal to or less than paying for the ring to be cleaned & polished once a year and a few sizings over the time-frame (as well as having the prongs holding the tiny side stones re-tipped every 5 years or so) then it is well worth it.

- Get your rings insured. Yes there are warranties out there from jewelry stores for diamonds and occasionally rings but they don't cover if your ring is lost, damaged beyond repair or stolen. Also be careful with the "due to negligence" fine writing in some warranties that allows them to not live up to the warranty (negligence pretty much means everything and anything you do to it).

- Don't forget wedding day jewelry. You may want pearls, earrings or pendants to accessorize with your dress. Also, you may find some really gorgeous and timeless gifts for your bridesmaids. I gave my bridesmaids different colored pearl bracelets as a gift and every once in a while I smile when I see them with it on.

- Guys put on a front that they don't care about jewelry or their bands and most of the time it is because they don't spend time looking at it in magazines or pinterest. Remind them that this is their ring and it should be something that they want to look at every day. There are tons of styles out there for gents bands and his personality is in one of those styles. Don't let him be frugal or cheap about his ring (cough, cough... $10 silicone band on Etsy). He deserves a quality ring that will last a lifetime as well!

💜 Put on your jewelry last when getting ready for the wedding. You don't want all of that hairspray covering up the shine from your diamonds.

Insider Secrets

💜 This is something that is going to be forever. Don't wait until the last minute to get your rings because your budget might take a hit and you'll be left with rings that either you won't like or are poorly made, aka cheap. Do you really want to spend more on drinks and food than something you will be wearing and looking at every day?

💜 The best time to get a more personalized experience at a jewelry store is during the week, usually Monday through Thursday, during the day. Try to make an appointment as well.

💜 The two biggest mistakes we have seen and regrets that we have heard from couples are these: 1. Treating the rings that you will wear every day for the rest of your lives as an afterthought. 2. Not having enough time to get the ring that you want in your size on Special Order.

💜 Speaking of sizing. It is imperative that you are sized correctly and surprisingly this does not happen all of the time in a jewelry store. Ask for a seasoned veteran or the jeweler to correctly size you. The sizer should go onto the finger smoothly and should be somewhat of a struggle when taking it off while going over the knuckle.

💜 If you are looking to create a custom ring from scratch, give yourself 2-3 months from start to finish. You will need to consult on the design, have a wax or CAD done and then approve or make changes to the wax or CAD & finally approve. This may take a month. After the approval they will begin the long and skilled process of making your ring which could take an additional 1-2 months depending on how many diamonds are being placed into it.

💜 Your rings are made of precious metals and diamonds. They will need to be maintained. White gold is not naturally white and will get a yellowish hue to it over time. You will need to have it polished and dipped. All precious metals will scratch and need to be polished. Platinum will get a grayish look to it from all of the tiny scratches, but a simple polishing will make it nice and bright again. Everything that comes in contact with your hand will end up underneath your diamond for some reason and a spa treatment in an ultrasonic machine, along with a steam, will make them shine once more. The tips of the prongs will wear down over time and need to be retipped with the same metal to keep the diamond from falling out. It's like a car engine, if you neglect it, bad things will happen.

"Don't wait until the last minute to get your rings because your budget might take a hit and you'll be left with rings that either you won't like or are poorly made, aka cheap."

Jewelry - To Do List

- [ ] _____
- [ ] _____
- [ ] _____
- [ ] _____
- [ ] _____
- [ ] _____
- [ ] _____
- [ ] _____
- [ ] _____
- [ ] _____
- [ ] _____
- [ ] _____
- [ ] _____
- [ ] _____
- [ ] _____
- [ ] _____
- [ ] _____
- [ ] _____

My Thoughts

Jeweler	Contact Name	Phone	Email	Jeweler On Site	His Band Price	Her Band Price	Day Of Jewelry	Do They Have A Warranty?	Notes

Notes

To-Dos & Schedule From 12 Months Out

To-Dos & Schedule From 12 Months Out

Lucy & I extended our timeline beyond 12 months because we wanted to be able to save as much money as possible and pay with cash wherever we could. Lucy is also Vietnamese and her tradition, similar to an Italian wedding, is to accept envelopes instead of presents. This also needed to be factored into our day of timeline. We went table to table and greeted the elders at the table with a thank you and poured them either a nicely aged bourbon or a very tasty dessert wine. Each table also could toast to us with the beverage of their choice or play a game before we received the envelopes. Let's just say they like to party! I'm surprised we made it all the way around standing up. There are many different ideas about when you should do certain tasks. This wedding timeline took into consideration about 30 different professional timelines as well as personal & professional experience. Ultimately, you should be able to adjust and add to it the way that works best for you.

12+ months out

- Enjoy being engaged before you start planning
- Budget
- Guest list
- Select an "around" date
- Wedding Bands
- Create a separate email address just for the wedding
- Select a wedding planner book
- Theme/Feel
- Select venue
- Select caterer

- ♥ Start looking for hotel blocks

11 months out

- ♥ Choose colors
- ♥ Select the people you want for your wedding party
- ♥ Brainstorm design
- ♥ Begin meeting with vendors
  - ◊ Planners/Coordinators
  - ◊ Caterers
  - ◊ Florist
  - ◊ Cake Artist
  - ◊ Ceremony Musicians
  - ◊ Officiant
  - ◊ Bartenders
  - ◊ Rentals
- ♥ Select photographer/videographer
- ♥ Select band or DJ

10 Months Out

- ♥ Wedding dress shopping
- ♥ Book hotel room blocks
- ♥ Wedding website
- ♥ Shop for invitations

9 Months Out

- ♥ Buy wedding dress
- ♥ Save The Dates
- ♥ Hair/Makeup/Lashes trial (great time to take photos after)
- ♥ Engagement Photos

8 Months Out

- ♥ Register for gifts
- ♥ Select Bridesmaids dresses (schedule fittings)
- ♥ Shop for florists

7 Months Out

- Research rehearsal dinner venue
- Hire ceremony musicians
- Order rental items
- Select Officiant

6 Months Out

- Select Lighting Technician (better yet a DJ with lighting services)
- Brainstorm honeymoon ideas

5 Months Out

- Book transportation
- Book honeymoon
- Select groom's clothing
- Premarital counseling/coaching

4 Months Out

- Tasting with caterer
- Select cake
- Select clothing for groomsmen (schedule fittings)
- Buy wedding day jewelry

3 Months Out

- Order invitations
- Create menu
- Brainstorm guest favors
- Select photo booth rental
- Brainstorm Bachelor/Bachelorette parties
- Select readings for ceremony
- Meet with Officiant
- Get going on DIY projects (sooner if possible)
- Book Hair/Makeup/Lash/Brow Artists

2 Months Out

- Send out invitations
- First dress fitting
- Select & book rehearsal dinner location
- Get marriage license
- Buy wedding party gifts
- Mock reception table set up with florist
- Give playlist to Band/DJ (as well as do not play list)
- Give song selections to ceremony musicians
- Buy smaller items
- The more risky venue booking! Waiting until two months before the wedding sounds scary, and it is, but it can save you up to 25% on the venue because they want it filled.
- Have Bachelor/Bachelorette parties

1 Month Out

- Assemble gift bags
- Pay vendors in full
- All RSVPs followed up & tallied
- Create & finalize seating chart
- Order/Make escort cards/place cards
- Final venue walk-through
- Create your wedding vows
- Create cash envelopes for vendor tips
- Create your wedding day timeline
- Break in wedding shoes
- Drive around the ceremony & reception neighborhood. If something comes up, you'll know where to send someone like the grocery store for lactose free, keto diet, vegan Vanessa's special meal. Or where to send someone for a special bottle of Mums for Uncle Larry's table because your cousin had one at her wedding last month and he keeps talking about it.
- Finish all non-perishable DIY projects

Final Week

- Refresh hair color
- Get eyebrows done
- Mani/Pedi
- Check in with all vendors
- Couples massage
- Make a must have photo list for photographer
- Final dress fitting
- Send timelines to all vendors
- Pack bags for wedding night/honeymoon
- Clean rings at jeweler
- Final calls to any VIPs or A list that did not RSVP
- Deliver final head count to caterer
- Practice your vows out loud
- Write your sweetheart a note
- Make an emergency kit. Advil, bobby pins, umbrella, safety pins, makeup wipes, chargers, etc. You know what to add.

Night Before Wedding

- Eat fresh & healthy meals
- Pack a small bag for personal items
- Drink water
- Go to sleep early
- Put things that need to go to the ceremony/reception site in your car if possible.

Morning Of Wedding

- Relax. No more worrying about logistics. Be in the moment with your sweetheart.
- Don't have anything on a to-do list for your wedding day. A good Wedding planner won't have anything on their list either.
- Eat a fresh, healthy breakfast.
- Did we mention water?
- Take dresses and suits/tuxedos out to have them air out and steamed if needed.
- Prepare for the photographer (give a list of things you'd like captured).

- ♥ Exchange notes with your sweetheart.
- ♥ Say thank you . . . to everyone.

Between The Ceremony & Reception

- ♥ Schedule some time for you and your sweetheart to be alone together. 30 minutes is a good rule of thumb. Have the transportation take you on a scenic drive. Go to a favorite quiet spot that you go to as a couple. Find a quiet area in the reception venue where you two can be alone (maybe 10 minutes of that with the photographer/videographer, the rest alone) and just enjoy the moment with each other.

Insider Secrets

- ♥ Pack some protein bars for the day of. You will be doing so many things you may forget to eat until your meal is served. Eat a protein bar. You don't want to be the star of the newest viral "passing-out on her wedding day" video.

"Having a plan is everything. There should be a general schedule, timeline and dates that things need to be completed by. This will make your wedding less stressful."

Timeline - To Do List

- [ ] _____
- [ ] _____
- [ ] _____
- [ ] _____
- [ ] _____
- [ ] _____
- [ ] _____
- [ ] _____
- [ ] _____
- [ ] _____
- [ ] _____
- [ ] _____
- [ ] _____
- [ ] _____
- [ ] _____
- [ ] _____
- [ ] _____
- [ ] _____
- [ ] _____

Timeline - To Do List

- [ ] _____
- [ ] _____
- [ ] _____
- [ ] _____
- [ ] _____
- [ ] _____
- [ ] _____
- [ ] _____
- [ ] _____
- [ ] _____
- [ ] _____
- [ ] _____
- [ ] _____
- [ ] _____
- [ ] _____
- [ ] _____
- [ ] _____
- [ ] _____
- [ ] _____

Timeline - To Do List

- [ ] _____
- [ ] _____
- [ ] _____
- [ ] _____
- [ ] _____
- [ ] _____
- [ ] _____
- [ ] _____
- [ ] _____
- [ ] _____
- [ ] _____
- [ ] _____
- [ ] _____
- [ ] _____
- [ ] _____
- [ ] _____
- [ ] _____
- [ ] _____
- [ ] _____

My Thoughts

Wedding Planner

Wedding Planner

You know that one friend who is always planning parties, loves helping others set up parties, is a project manager at work or simply knows how to coax people into getting things done? Perhaps they could gift you their talents for the day of the wedding or even the month of the wedding. We asked a cousin who is a phenomenal planner, organizes home schooling for groups and coordinates special events to be our voice on the wedding day. Our venue contact gave us some spectacular tips as well. If you know that you will be using a wedding planner, put your feelers out there with friends, family or co-workers who have been married in the last few years. They may put you on to a phenomenal planner who never would have caught your attention.

What To Ask A Wedding Planner/Coordinator

- Do you charge hourly, by a percentage of our budget or a flat fee?
- Do you handle payment for all vendors?
- Do you receive commission from any of the vendors that you will be recommending or using?
- What is the biggest wedding you have worked before?
- What is the way you communicate with us throughout the process?
- How do you select vendors and how will we be involved?
- Will you go outside of your preferred list of vendors if we already had some in mind?
- How many meetings will we have together throughout this process?
- How would you describe your style both working with us and working with vendors on our behalf?
- When will you arrive and when will you leave on the wedding day?
- What will you and your team wear to the ceremony & reception?

- Do you do everything from table assignments to tastings to takedown and everything in between no matter how small?
- How many people from your team will be working the day of our wedding?
- Full Service means different things to different Wedding Planners. Is full service really everything that we would need done?
- What would we be responsible for throughout the planning process?
- Now that we have explained our style and vision for the wedding, what ideas came to mind?
- How do you make sure the wedding timeline is adhered to?
- How do you deal with wedding day disasters?
- Do you create alternate plans for inclement weather when weddings are outdoors?

Things You Haven't Thought About

- Day Of Wedding Planner
- Month Of Wedding Planner
- Full-Service Coordination
- Budget Development
- Timeline Creation
- Rehearsal Coordination
- Wedding Day Set Up & Take Down Management

Tips & Tricks

- Be as clear as possible about your opinions, vision and expectations. They can't read your mind.
- If you have a parent that needs to be involved in every detail but you have a wedding planner, find a way to let the parent(s) know that you want the professional to make decisions and you'd like the family to relax and enjoy the moment. Your wedding planner would LOVE to say this . . . but it can't come from them.
- If your parents are paying for your wedding, your wedding planner is going to listen to them more than they listen to you. Sounds harsh and unfair, but that's how it works unless expressed otherwise by the parent.
- Make sure everything that was offered is in the contract. If you don't see it, have them add it. After you secure a wedding planner or coordinator they should be doing the same level of scrutiny for all other vendors.

♥ Communication is key when it comes to planning a wedding. If your communication styles are not in sync with your wedding planner then you may want to interview others who you have a better communication vibe with.

♥ Wedding planners want the best for you and your special day, however, sometimes what you are asking for (especially if it is last minute) just can't be done. They are working within your budget to find your vision. Just because your wedding planner shuts an idea down doesn't mean they aren't on your side.

♥ Don't place your wedding planner in the middle of an argument about a decision between you and your sweetheart or a family member. They are not Judge Judy and shouldn't be expected to play referee.

♥ Being kind to all of your vendors from introduction to the wedding day will get you the best of their ability and possibly beyond.

♥ You are not required to feed all of your vendors the same meal that you are feeding your guests. Find an alternative through your caterer that will cost little but still be a tasty and filling meal to keep them going.

♥ If you have attended a wedding in the last 12 months that you really enjoyed, talk to the couple and see if they have any tips or tricks for you. They may also have some vendors that you could end up using.

♥ You actually have a ceremony too, not just the party at the reception. Make sure you focus just as intently on the time that you exchange vows and say I Do.

♥ Make sure your wedding rehearsal dinner isn't a party. The last thing you want is little sleep and large hangovers for the big day.

Insider Secrets

♥ See if your wedding planner is comfortable with adding late fees to vendor contracts. That's right! Late fees!! Contracts are both ways. If the vendor is late, they should have a fee deducted from the payment you made that would need to be returned to your card within a certain number of business days.

♥ Some coordinators will have an hourly fee for consultation. You can actually use their expertise for an hour with what you have planned yourself to see if there is anything that may have been overlooked.

♥ Make sure the planner or coordinator is not 90 percent focused on the reception with a little bit on the Ceremony. The ceremony includes your vows, the first look and is typically more intimate for the two of you. The ceremony also sets the tone for the rest of the day. Don't give it a little attention, give it as much attention as your reception.

- Wedding planners hate Pinterest. Just thought you'd like to know.
- Pinterest is great and all, but it will also drive you crazy. Especially if you keep looking at it after decisions have been made. You'll second guess yourself. Consider your Pinterest board as a guide rather than the exact wedding you are going to have. Half of the time those aren't even real weddings, they are photoshoots.
- Be careful. A "highly recommended" vendor from the wedding planner might actually be the highest paid commission or kick-back to the planner. Check out their recommendations before you give the go-ahead to book.
- If there is one thing you should listen to, it is this: don't do a cash bar. The wedding reception drinks and food is all about your guests. They shouldn't have to break out the wallet for their whiskey on the rocks. Find a way to include the drinks.
- Your guests care more about being comfortable, having a good time and being able to get a drink fairly easily. Believe it or not they won't remember the hand crafted table card holders made from wine corks. Prioritize your energy and money.
- Prepare for the worst and you will have a glorious day. Every wedding has something that goes wrong. Most of the time you won't even know or care. Other times you may literally have a disaster. Like the time I was at a beautiful outdoor/indoor wedding when a tornado decided to show up. There really wasn't a plan for that and everyone huddled together in a hallway while the bride cried her eyes out. Now it is a memorable story for them to tell rather than a super stressful moment from their wedding day.
- Wedding planning is about organization. If you are bad at organization, you may want to skip a full out DIY wedding. One way you can organize is through our amazing Ultimate Wedding Planner Secret sheets, some of which are printed in this book under each section or you can get the Excel/Google sheets from us that calculate and organize everything for you all in one place. It also offers a few different types of visual timelines because your timeline is your everything. You can get it at https://www.infinancer.com/weddings
- We've said this before but . . . read . . . every . . . contract. Every single one. Every word.

Coordinator - To Do List

- [ ] _____
- [ ] _____
- [ ] _____
- [ ] _____
- [ ] _____
- [ ] _____
- [ ] _____
- [ ] _____
- [ ] _____
- [ ] _____
- [ ] _____
- [ ] _____
- [ ] _____
- [ ] _____
- [ ] _____
- [ ] _____
- [ ] _____
- [ ] _____
- [ ] _____

My Thoughts

Vendor Role	Business Name	Contact Name	Phone	Email	Cost	Deposit Due	Balance Due	Form Of Payment	Notes

Venue

Venue

We have a friend who had one of the most beautiful weddings we have attended. It was in the Japanese Friendship Garden at Balboa Park in San Diego. Imagine walking among perfectly manicured bonsai trees, tranquil bridges over koi ponds, waterfalls and flowers of all colors with Japanese architecture perfectly mingled in amongst it all. In the evening, the lovely paper lanterns and stringed lights lit up the reception. It was truly memorable. No matter what style you are going for, the venue will be the main piece of the puzzle for how your vision comes to life.

What To Ask The Venue

- ♥ How many people does this venue accommodate?
- ♥ Can we have the ceremony & reception here? Are there additional costs for that?
- ♥ How many hours are included? What are the overage fees?
- ♥ How much time are we given for the rehearsal?
- ♥ What is the contingency plan for inclement weather?
- ♥ Is liability insurance included?
- ♥ What time can my vendors begin arriving?
- ♥ Do you have a list of the decor we can use as part of the venue package?
- ♥ Can confetti or flower petals be used? You'd be surprised at how many say no. If the answer is no . . . . bubbles. Yes. Bubbles.
- ♥ Do you provide heaters/umbrellas (outdoors)?
- ♥ Is there on site coordination? Are outside coordinators/planners allowed?
- ♥ Is there security included?
- ♥ Where are wedding gifts stored and secured? Can you pick them up the next day?

- Do you have a generator for power outages?
- What separate spaces are included?
- Do you have a sound system? Microphones?
- How many restrooms are available?
- Are there events happening at the venue on the same day?
- Where is the kitchen in relation to the reception site?
- If the ceremony & reception are held at the same place, how does the conversion take place?
- How many people can sit comfortably at one table?
- What are the closest accommodations?
- When do we need to confirm guest numbers by and what if those guest numbers change?
- Where do the guests park? How many spots are there?

Things You Haven't Thought About

- Ceremony site fees
- Church donation
- Officiant fee
- Ceremony accessories (flower girl basket, unity candle, ring pillow, etc.)
- Additional rentals not provided by the caterer (tables, chair covers, etc.)
- Dance floor rental
- Parking fees
- Insurance fees
- Service fees
- Security (if required)

Tips & Tricks

- Hold your wedding ceremony & reception in one place if at all possible. Transportation fees and vendor fees may decrease significantly because of it.
- Find a venue that lets you bring your own alcohol. You can purchase the alcohol yourself, control the cost and get a licensed and insured bartender or two to serve it up for less than most venues offer.
- Find natural decorations as accents such as pinecones or small branches. A touch of spray paint in the hue of your wedding colors and you'll be surprised how something you find in nature can make a visual difference.
- Take advantage of holidays where your venue may already be decorated for it.
- Venue prices seem to magically increase when a wedding is involved. Some

say this is fact, others say this is fiction. When shopping around and getting quotes, just tell them that you are planning an event. Don't go overboard though. If they ask if this is for a wedding, don't continue on with the "large event" line, just be honest. Especially if you are having this event on a Saturday night in July. They know.

- ♥ Always ask about hidden fees that may pop up. If Uncle Pauly has a bit too much Peachy Canyon wine and stains a carpet . . . you may want to know ahead of time what that would cost you.
- ♥ Decorate with a combination of candles, plants, herbs and flowers to reduce dollars and add more scents to the event. See what we did there?
- ♥ Check out local government buildings or historic buildings. They may offer the place up for substantially less. There is a gorgeous Mayor's Balcony at a city hall in California that rents for just $1,000 and allows for up to 100 guests. The acoustics of that building is something else too!
- ♥ Ever thought about a small hometown brewery or distillery? Need food to go with that? There might be a very desirable food truck that you can lock down as well.
- ♥ Going all out? How about custom bottles of wine with your guests' names on them (couples get one bottle). It serves as a name placement and parting gift. That is, unless they don't pop it open during the reception.
- ♥ A high quality venue rarely requires an outside wedding planner.
- ♥ Ask for dates that may be available that could save you some money. Especially if the venue is just over or right at your budgeted levels.
- ♥ Ask about everything that is included in the booking of your venue. Also ask them if there are things that are available that you may not see in your tour. Do they have extra loveseats for guests to relax in? Will that cost less than renting & delivering/pick-up from an outside vendor? They may have specialty decorations that will cost less than renting. Think outside the box here.
- ♥ Use photos as table designations. Childhood photos, High School photos, early, middle or current relationship photos can all help differentiate tables for your guests.
- ♥ You can have your favorite books as part of the decor on the tables. Have an empty bowl on the table as well. The name cards can be placed in the bowl to see who wins the book. Self improvement or classic books are awesome for this.
- ♥ Make your own confetti with old, dried flowers. Removing dead flowers from work? Dry them out? Did your sweetheart give you some flowers and they are on their last leg? Dry them out. Tell friends and family you

would be grateful for their dead flowers too. Yes, they might think you're weird until you explain why.

- If you are buying items or DIYing things for the wedding, reconsider Bride & Groom on decorations. Try Mr. & Mrs. or your initials instead. Why? Because those can be repurposed as decor around your house.

Insider Secrets

- Off days, times and seasons will allow you to book a dreamy place at a substantial discount.
- Choose a naturally beautiful location that will require less decoration.
- If you live in a big (and expensive) city, consider going to the outskirts or countryside. Venues will not only be more scenic and picturesque, they'll be less expensive.
- Don't create an alternate universe in terms of style/look/feel for your wedding. Just because Pinterest is pummeling you with new modern-themed trends doesn't mean your true style of country chic needs to be ditched for what is in. Your wedding is a reflection of you as a couple. Keep that at the forefront.
- If you have a place that you like, but want a few days to read the contract, ask for a "soft hold". The vendor will pencil you in for the date and call you if someone else is interested in those dates.
- Ask what you will have to rent outside of what the venue offers. They may have a connection for what you need at a discounted price.
- Some of the least expensive venues could also be the most beautiful. Think museums, a park, a historic library or historic building, golf course, garden, beach, aquariums, yachts for rent, schools, theaters, farms, etc.

Venue - To Do List

- [ ] _____
- [ ] _____
- [ ] _____
- [ ] _____
- [ ] _____
- [ ] _____
- [ ] _____
- [ ] _____
- [ ] _____
- [ ] _____
- [ ] _____
- [ ] _____
- [ ] _____
- [ ] _____
- [ ] _____
- [ ] _____
- [ ] _____
- [ ] _____
- [ ] _____

My Thoughts

Venue	Contact Name	Phone	Email	Capacity	Number Of Hours	Cost Of Venue	Cost Per Person	Minimum Food & Beverage	Notes

Notes

Engagement Party

Engagement Party

There are many types of engagement parties. Traditional, cultural, formal, casual and even themed engagement parties. We had a traditional Vietnamese engagement ceremony that is almost like a wedding ceremony. My family welcomed Adam's family wearing the traditional áo dài and presenting gifts covered in a red cloth that has been in the family for generations. Once inside, the family members were formally introduced and each of our parents said their well-wishes. Adam then poured tea for our parents. Funny story about that. Many of the guests thought it was so cute because the teapot lid was rattling while Adam poured the tea and they thought he was nervous, but that wasn't why. The ceramic teapot was so hot that it was burning his hands while he was pouring it. He endured the pain to complete the traditional pour.

What To Ask Yourselves

- When are we going to have the engagement party?
- Who should we invite?
- Are there any traditions that we are going to incorporate during the engagement party?
- Is this something a planner will coordinate by itself or as part of the wedding package?
- Is it going to be casual or formal?
- Who will be paying for it?
- What is the budget?
- Where will it be hosted?
- Do we want a theme or special decor?
- What are we going to wear?

- Is our photographer going to attend and capture the moment?
- What special touches do we want to add?

Things You Haven't Thought About

- Invitations
- Attire
- Cultural Traditions
- Toasts
- Full Meal or Bites
- Photos
- Special Activities

Tips & Tricks

- Traditionally, the bride's parents host the engagement party. If you aren't traditional, do it your way.
- Invitations should mirror the type of party you are throwing. The more formal the engagement party, the more formal the invitation should be.
- What you wear and the place you choose to host should be in alignment with how formal or informal your engagement party is.
- People do buy gifts for engagement parties. If you register, think about low priced to medium priced gifts as the wedding gifts may be more expensive.
- Assign day-of duties just as you would for your wedding.
- Engagement parties could be anything from backyard barbeques to cocktail parties to country club formals.
- You may also consider dinner at your favorite restaurant, a snazzy hotel suite or a picnic in a scenic outdoor setting.
- Your guest list for the engagement party will be more intimate than that of your wedding. The closest of friends and family.
- Your parents and the both of you should greet all guests as they arrive.
- Unlike the wedding, open mics are OK for toasts. You should begin with each set of parents followed by the couple.
- Giving the parents and the host a gift is a good way to set the tone for the evening.
- Most engagement parties are from 2-4 hours.
- Think about having a menu that has each of your favorite foods and a favorite food that the both of you like. It's a great conversation starter.

- One of the funnest ideas we have heard of for an engagement party is where the couple recreated their first date. Admit it. It's genius!
- It's okay to have themed engagement parties and/or fun games. Imagine the possibilities!!! Movie Theater, Wine & Cheese, Poker Party, Brunch, Bonfire or even a group outdoor activity if that's your jam.
- Everyone is going to want to know how the proposal took place. Having a video or slideshow with pictures throughout the relationship and including the engagement might help you from having to repeat the same story 30 times.
- Have printed signs with stories from your relationship as well as the proposal and pictures of you throughout the event as decor.

Insider Secrets

- You should have your engagement party within the first 3 months of getting engaged. The closer to your engagement the better.
- You typically invite those who attend the engagement party to the wedding, however, not everyone invited to the wedding doesn't get invited to the engagement party.
- Make sure your invitation suggests to the guests what they should wear. If you don't, Jermaine might show up in a full on Tux and a bottle of Clicquot while Javier shows up in shorts and a t-shirt with a 6 pack of craft beer.
- Each of your parents should meet before the actual engagement party so there is familiarity for the actual event.
- Decide on the menu early as this will more than likely be the largest expense of the party.
- Send thank you cards with handwritten, personal messages to those that attend.
- Think about music. It's definitely OK to have a playlist and a bluetooth speaker or even a friend who has a band.
- You can have more than one party. Adam set up a celebration the same day he proposed which started at a wine bar with a meal and ended at a club (all in the same hotel). We also had the aforementioned traditional Vietnamese engagement party. You may want to have a party with friends and a separate party with family.
- Memorize this for when everyone asks you about the wedding: "We are just enjoying the moment of getting engaged and will definitely send you the save the date as soon as we start planning". If you don't, you can

expect 50 different ideas for your wedding.

- ♥ The planning of the engagement party should not be stressful. Quick, yet meaningful decisions will be paramount to your sanity.
- ♥ Save your best ideas for the wedding. The engagement party is not the place to show off what your wedding day is going to look or feel like.

"One of the most fun ideas we have heard of for an engagement party is where the couple recreated their first date. Admit it. It's genius!"

Engagement Party - To Do List

- [ ] _____
- [ ] _____
- [ ] _____
- [ ] _____
- [ ] _____
- [ ] _____
- [ ] _____
- [ ] _____
- [ ] _____
- [ ] _____
- [ ] _____
- [ ] _____
- [ ] _____
- [ ] _____
- [ ] _____
- [ ] _____
- [ ] _____
- [ ] _____
- [ ] _____

My Thoughts

Hotels
For
Guests

Hotels For Guests

So, we have a confession to make. For our own wedding we didn't really check to see what other events were happening in the city or reserve a hotel block for out of town guests. Big mistake. One of the biggest conventions, Comic-Con in San Diego, took almost all of the rooms away and a lot of our out of town guests ended up at a hotel about 40 minutes away (in good traffic). Luckily, it was right on the beach. Learn from our mistakes, check out hotel room blocks early and make sure you know what events might be happening in the city.

What To Ask The Hotel

- Do you offer a courtesy room block?
- What is the maximum number of rooms allowed for a courtesy block?
- What other events are you having at the hotel the week of my wedding?
- Is there a room minimum in order to secure a block?
- Is there an attrition clause?
- What is the cutoff date for guests to book rooms by?
- What amenities are included?
- How do guests book their room block? Will there be an online code or do they have to call in?
- Do you provide transportation to and from the hotel?
- Can rooms be booked after the cutoff date at the discounted rate if there is still availability?
- Can more rooms be added if needed?
- How can I deliver welcome gifts to the rooms?
- Will there be one single person that we will be working with or will we have different people answering questions and assisting?

- What extras can you provide in the room block package?
- Is there complimentary breakfast included? What other amenities will my guests be able to enjoy?
- Do you offer a complimentary suite for the bride & groom?
- Will I receive a rooming list of my guests?
- Will my guests be placed in the same area of the hotel?
- Is early check in and late check out an option?

Things You Haven't Thought About

- When to reserve a room block by
- Whether you will be granted access for welcome gifts
- What happens if all of the rooms are not booked
- Negotiating perks
- How other events might affect the price & availability of room blocks.
- Do we want to hold pre or post wedding events at the hotel?
- Thank you cards for the hotel staff members that assisted you the most. You may even want to give them any extra welcome gift bags that weren't handed out as a thank you.

Tips & Tricks

- Major events happening on or around your wedding date means price hikes for hotel rooms.
- Place your hotel block information (including instructions on how to book within the block) on your wedding website.
- You should book your hotel block at least 4-8 months in advance if possible.
- Make sure the hotel(s) you choose are easily accessible not only to the wedding ceremony & reception sites, but also to the airport. Try your hardest to stay within a 30 minute drive of each.
- If you are staying at the hotel on the wedding night as well, negotiate a free upgrade for your room when choosing the hotel.
- Be very conservative with the number of rooms you want to block. If the block fills up, the hotel should be more than happy to add more rooms to the block.
- If you have a lot of out of town guests coming in, try blocking 2-3 hotels with different price points. Make sure enough people will utilize these blocks as you may find yourself being charged for unused rooms down the line.
- If you don't want to book blocks in different hotels, create a list of other

accommodations that range in price for guests that may be on a budget or may want to splurge.

- The more room blocks in different hotels you have, the more spread out your guests will be and the more places you will have to go to deliver welcome gifts. You'll also need to figure out more transportation options.
- You should know each hotel's check in and check out times just in case your guests ask.
- Auto-schedule email reminders to out of town guests. The first one should be right after booking the block(s) with the information. The next email should be a month before the cut-off. The last email should be a week or two before the cut-off.
- 1-2 weeks before the cut-off date, ask the hotel for a copy of the room list and send a reminder to out of town guests who may not have booked yet.
- 1-2 days before check-in, drop off the welcome gifts if the hotel is placing it in the rooms for you.
- See if you can negotiate a complimentary room for your 1 year anniversary with the room block.
- Try to start your wedding at least an hour after check-in time. Hotels can't guarantee early check-ins because they may have unforeseen circumstances in getting rooms ready. Suggest to your guests, however, that they request early check-in at the time of booking.
- If you have transportation from the hotel to the wedding venue included in your negotiations, try to have two times for departures and include them on your invitations and reminder emails.
- See if an extra itinerary can be handed to each guest in your block upon check-in. People always seem to lose the most important information while traveling.

Insider Secrets

- A closed or guaranteed block typically requires a deposit and a minimum amount of rooms must be booked or you will pay a fee. Use this if you are very, very sure you will book all the rooms. Otherwise this is a last resort.
- Open or Courtesy Blocks will have a cutoff date and also require a deposit. There is a small, or possibly no penalty for unsold rooms in the block. This type of block is especially good if you can add rooms after completing the block or are considering having blocks at multiple hotels.

- For your contract, you will want to know what certain phrases are. Attrition rate is the percentage of rooms that must be filled. Allowable shrinkage is the percentage of rooms that go unbooked. Mitigation or Resell clause is where the hotel must try to book unused rooms to other guests so you are not penalized for them.

- For negotiation, you'll want to know what they are talking about which will let them know you can't be taken advantage of. If they don't bring up the deposit amount, cut-off date, the cancellation policy and some of the more intricate contract details then you certainly should bring them up.

- Some hotels charge for extras, see if your hotel block will provide benefits such as free parking, free wi-fi, late check outs because of hangovers and even free upgrades for guests.

- When negotiating room blocks, never accept the first offer. You aren't just negotiating rates, you are negotiating additional perks as well. If you are not good at negotiating or are timid, have someone else take charge of this. Just make sure they aren't too cut-throat. You need to maintain a good relationship with the hotel.

- The further out you begin shopping hotels and negotiating, the more leverage you have. They probably haven't booked many rooms yet and this is a way for them to guarantee a large number of bookings.

- Hotels can block rooms up to a year in advance.

- See if you can add Shoulder Days to the block. Some guests may arrive a few days before and/or leave a few days after the wedding.

- Give the hotel 3 copies of your schedule so they know what to expect. Why 3? Extras in case one is lost or if there are more than one front desk clerks.

Hotel - To Do List

- [ ] _____
- [ ] _____
- [ ] _____
- [ ] _____
- [ ] _____
- [ ] _____
- [ ] _____
- [ ] _____
- [ ] _____
- [ ] _____
- [ ] _____
- [ ] _____
- [ ] _____
- [ ] _____
- [ ] _____
- [ ] _____
- [ ] _____
- [ ] _____
- [ ] _____

My Thoughts

Hotel	Contact Name	Phone	Email	Group Room Rate	Min. # Guaranteed Rooms	Cost If All Rooms Not Booked	Perks	Notes

Notes

Caterer

Caterer

Think back to all of the weddings that you have been to. Was there a culinary experience that stands out? Do most blend in with each other? Would you like chicken or steak ma'am? The most memorable food experiences we have been blessed to have while two people share their love for each other are the ones that are unexpected. Cultural flare always hits the spot. Outside the box food stations seem to endlessly impress. Menus that you'd never think would be at a wedding reception are sure to make your senses smile. Even homemade meals prepared by friends and family can leave a lasting impression.

What To Ask A Caterer

- Do you have any other obligations that day?
- Can you tell us about the experience you provide guests?
- How much space do you need at the venue?
- When is the latest I can give a final head count?
- What is included and what might cost extra?
- How long does your service typically take?
- What are your most popular dishes?
- Do you offer tastings? Is there a charge for it?
- What types of meal service do you offer (service, buffet, stations, etc.)?
- Where does the food come from (frozen, organic, local, etc.)?
- Can you tell us about your staff & servers?
- What color & style options do you offer?
- Do you provide all of the rentals that will be needed?
- How will the food be prepared the day of the wedding?

- Do you allow for custom menus?
- Can you accommodate dietary restrictions for select guests?
- Can you handle last minute requests?
- Can you do theme menus?
- Are there childrens options & if so how much?
- Are vendor meals discounted?
- Do you charge cake cutting fees?
- What is your cleanup policy?
- Have you worked with any other wedding vendors in the past that stood out to you and would refer?
- Do you provide bartenders & bars? Drink Stations?
- Can you accommodate specialty drinks?
- Can we provide the alcohol or do you provide select brands?
- Is the champagne toast included?
- What do the servers wear?
- What is the ratio of servers to guests?
- How do you handle gratuity for your staff?

Things You Haven't Thought About

- Cocktail Hour Drinks
- Reception Drinks
- Specialty Drinks
- Bartender Service
- Coffee/Tea
- Non Alcoholic Beverages
- Glassware
- Signage/Drink Menu
- Corkage Fees
- Liquor License/Insurance Fees
- Tips
- Tasting Appointment
- Rehearsal Dinner
- Service Staff
- Service Utensils such as plates, silverware, platters, bowls & glassware.
- Adding your vendors to the total number of plates you are purchasing
- Tables/Chairs/Linens if the venue does not provide them
- Service Charges
- Make your own dessert bar
- Ask the caterer to send leftovers home with guests or to a food bank

after the event is over.

♥ If you have a caterer in mind or a friend that is a chef or owns a restaurant who will be your go-to vendor, make sure the venue allows outside vendors before you book. The last thing you want to do is book a reception site only to find out your friend who's already planning your wedding day meal can't do his or her thing.

Tips & Tricks

♥ Consider a local restaurant instead of a caterer.

♥ Close the bar an hour early. It saves you on time and gives people a chance to reconcile their overconsumption.

♥ There are good, low cost wines out there. Start tasting Trader Joes wines or wines you find at the grocery store to find the ones you like best.

♥ Have you heard of the wedding brunch? Getting married in the morning just might be your thing.

♥ Beer, Wine & a signature drink or two will cut costs (especially if you can bring it yourself.

♥ Consider stations instead of full service.

♥ Not having alcohol at your wedding? There are some really fancy tea stations that can be rented.

♥ The rule of thumb for bartenders is one bartender for every 40 adult guests.

♥ Edible party favors not only are tasty, they are easy to take home too.

♥ How timely potential vendors are in their responses often is indicative of how responsive they will be if you select them. Don't be surprised if Ruffalo's Chicken Gizzards is 15 minutes late to service and doesn't let the coordinator know that they ran out of something if it took them 2 weeks to respond to your voicemail and a month to answer questions you sent.

♥ If there is a way to tie in your wedding theme to the menu . . . do it!

♥ Have you thought about a Midnight snack? Well, it doesn't really have to be at midnight but imagine having cocktail hour, an appetizer station and then a meal with dancing and a big party with drinking to follow. Now imagine one last tasty treat for your guests at the perfect time, late into the party.

♥ Tip the person who brings you your food at the tasting. They're working.

♥ Trends you might be interested in: Food Trucks, Drink Pairings, Charcuterie boards on steroids, Food Stations, Alcoholic beverage tastings, cigar rolling stations.

- DIY catering is fun, creates memories with those that help and shows true love for your guests to put that type of effort into it. On the flip side, consider the time and effort you have to put into it as well as the logistics let alone if there is a mishap and you end up… well… catering because of it.
- If you're having a cocktail hour, spend a little bit more here as most guests see this as the best part of a wedding.

Insider Secrets

- Few guests actually drink the champagne for your toast. Instead of Champagne, try sparkling wine or a prosecco. They probably wouldn't mind toasting with their beverage of choice either.
- Instead of having servers walking around with hors d'oeuvres, think about an appetizer station that guests can go to at their leisure during cocktail hour. This will minimize your staff fees.
- You'll find many vendors have a lot of add-ons that quickly add up. Opt out of bread baskets for tables. It will reduce your cost and the people attending your wedding will actually eat their meal instead of filling up on bread & butter.
- Don't forget to make sure your caterer is planning for additional plates, forks & napkins for the cake cutting.
- You have a vision for the meal, but you can't get lobster and steak plus 4 other courses for $75 a plate. Tell the caterers that you prefer what your vision is but let them know you are open to a creative menu that fits within your budget. You may be surprised at how amazing their options are without breaking the bank.
- Be on time for your tasting, come hungry and don't show up with 8 other people. Typically this is for you and your sweetheart and sometimes a few other people (like mom & dad if they're paying for the wedding). Ask the caterer first if you plan to have more people and if there would be an additional cost.
- Caterers don't make everything from scratch and preparing offsite vs onsite can make a big difference.
- Fluctuating food prices can severely affect the overall cost. Inflation? Price increase. A freeze that wiped out crops? Price increase. A fire at a major processing plant? Price increase. Asking for mango flavored rice topped with rambutan & durian inside of a sculptured ice bowl in

August? Price increase.

 Don't be afraid to politely move away from a certain dish that was supposed to be on the menu because you didn't like it at the tasting. The dish can be changed.

"Few guests actually drink the champagne for your toast. Instead of Champagne, try sparkling wine or a prosecco. They probably wouldn't mind toasting with their beverage of choice either."

Caterer - To Do List

My Thoughts

Caterer	Contact Name	Phone	Email	Main Entree Per Person	Beverage Per Person	Appetizer Per Person	Estimated Total	Notes

Notes

Stationery

Stationery

For the wedding invitation you may choose to pull out all the stops which means customizing an outer envelope, an inner envelope, an invitation card, the reception card, a detailed map (directions) card, the guest's RSVP card with self addressed and stamped envelope, a hotel block card and lastly a belly band. All closed up with a wax seal of course. On the other hand, your potential guests probably won't be fazed if you send out a link to your wedding site that has all of the information. The cutest, yet time-consuming idea that we have seen were invitation videos that were custom made for each and every guest and sent with a link to RSVP.

What To Ask Yourself & Stationery Professionals

- Do we want to DIY, have them professionally designed or a hybrid version of both?
- What is included in the wedding invitation packages you provide?
- Are the packages customizable?
- How do you create an invitation that is unique to us?
- What printing method is being used?
- Do you address the invitations for us? How do you do this (printed, calligraphy, etc.)?
- What about other stationary needs like table names/numbers, place cards, programs & others?
- How early in advance do we need to order the package?
- How long does it take to print these?
- Will you send me a fully completed sample first to approve? If so, have about 10 friends and family members check the proof before approving it.
- If there are errors in the printing or mistakes from the method of

printing, what is the process to correct it and how long will it take?

♥ Is there a deposit due or do we have to pay in full?

Things You Haven't Thought About

♥ Engagement Party invitations & Thank You Cards
♥ Bridal Shower Invitations & Thank You Cards
♥ Bachelorette/Bachelor Party Invitations
♥ Rehearsal Dinner Invitations
♥ Next Day Brunch invitations
♥ Postage
♥ RSVP postage
♥ Labels
♥ Wax Seal Kit
♥ Wedding Ceremony Programs
♥ Wedding Reception Menu
♥ Beverage Menu
♥ Favor Tags
♥ Place Cards
♥ Station Labels (Deserts, Appetizers, etc)
♥ Escort Cards
♥ Table Cards
♥ Thank You Cards
♥ Welcome Signs
♥ Guest Book
♥ Seating Chart
♥ Timeline Signs
♥ Gift Table Signage

Tips & Tricks

♥ Figure out what cards you want to include or combine in your invitation suite.
♥ If you are doing welcome baskets for out of town guests you will want to print out name tags for those guests.
♥ Get a free website to cut down on save the dates and invitations. Send traditional invitations to the closest of friends and family and for other guests send a link to the website or a postcard referring to it to reduce costs.

- Create a save the date video instead of sending cards. If you really want to take it to the next level, personalize each one.
- Not every person invited to the wedding needs a program. Print them out based on 1 per couple or family instead. Of course, the single studs and princesses will need their own unless they share with someone they connect with. Now that would be a story!!!
- Instead of printing out entrance welcomes and canvas photos, see if a local artist can create a custom mural for you with chalk, paint or whatever they specialize in.
- You can have a logo designed for as little as $5 or even find free ones on some sites. Find a logo specifically for your wedding and put them on everything from signs to favors to invites to menus and more.
- Number your invitations on a small corner before sending them out and put that number next to the names of the people in your planner. If someone forgets to write their name on the RSVP or the envelope you received is lost in the pile, you'll be able to look back at your notes and know who it is from.
- Have you ever heard of a vow booklet? They are super pretty and you can find them at all different price ranges. They also happen to be a tad more chic than a piece of paper or a notecard wouldn't you say?
- Spice up your reminder emails, DMs or text messages with memes. Yes, memes. There is science behind how they stimulate the brain.
- Test out the pens you will use for the guestbook in advance. You don't want to put out some duds and have a mad dash for a pen in the middle of guests arriving.
- Puns are fun.
- Asking a question on the RSVP is fun too! What is their favorite place to travel to, beverage or dance song would all be great questions to read when you receive them back.
- Try to send your save the dates 8-12 months out and invitations at least 2-4 months out.
- We all know that the stylish wedding script is romantic and beautiful... just make sure it prints well and can be read in the color of card stock and ink you select.
- Custom ink colors, handwritten calligraphy, belly bands and envelope liners can add up. Upgrades are nice, but if you are staying within a budget or need to move some stationary budget elsewhere, you may want to skip them.
- Having a bespoke wedding? Consider a bespoke invitation. This goes for any style. Remember though, your wedding style may change so don't be

upset if you send out a bespoke invitation suite and you end up having a city cocktail party wedding.

♥ Your guest book doesn't actually have to be a book. One of the cutest things we have seen was different shaped thin pieces of wood that the guests wrote their name and a note on which was then dropped into a slot at the top of a large picture frame that the couple would be hanging in their house.

♥ Keeping with the same thought of cute ideas that don't necessarily need to be a printed item. One wedding had an old reclaimed window frame with the windows still intact and each frame had the different table names and who was assigned to them.

Insider Secrets

♥ Did you know that square invitations will cost you more to mail out than rectangular ones? They are considered odd shaped and non-machinable and have to be processed by hand. Which means more money for processing & postage per envelope. True story!

♥ Naming your tables can help your guests find their tables with ease. Name each table after a special place that you and your sweetheart have been to or that means something to you. Was your first kiss on the cliffs of La Jolla overlooking the ocean? Name one of the tables La Jolla. Make a table card with the name, a picture and a short note on why La Jolla is special to the two of you. Adam did this for our wedding and I loved it!

♥ Combine your escort cards with your menu. A personalized menu with their name on top will cut stationary costs significantly.

♥ Send your invites out on a Wednesday. This way your potential guests will receive them on the weekend where they have more time to RSVP right away.

♥ Give yourself about a one month window to receive all RSVPs by. Deadlines are important here so you can provide the final headcount to the vendors you are working with.

♥ Are you all about technology . . . create a QR code for your invitation that sends them directly to your RSVP page or wedding website.

♥ Outside wedding? Avoid tri-fold escort cards. Wind and these types of cards are mortal enemies and will battle it out more than likely on the floor of your reception site instead of playing nice on the table.

♥ Most people generally don't care about wedding invitations. Make a really special one for you, your parents, grandparents and wedding party and cut costs on the rest.

- ♥ Don't forget to let your guests know, typically in the invitation, what the dress code will be (black tie, casual, cocktail style, etc.).
- ♥ Place your registry or gift suggestions like money envelopes or honeymoon contributions on your website, not your invitations. Place the wedding website on the save the dates.
- ♥ Buy more invitations than you need, you never know when that glass of wine decides to spill on your favorite sister's invitation. Unless she'll get a kick out of getting it this way.
- ♥ Digital & Offset printing is less expensive than Letterpress or Engraving.
- ♥ Never leave your guests guessing. From save the date to invitation to wedding signs throughout the venue they should know exactly where to go and what to look forward to.

"Did you know that square invitations will cost you more to mail out than rectangular ones? They are considered odd shaped and non-machinable and have to be processed by hand."

Stationery - To Do List

- [ ] _____
- [ ] _____
- [ ] _____
- [ ] _____
- [ ] _____
- [ ] _____
- [ ] _____
- [ ] _____
- [ ] _____
- [ ] _____
- [ ] _____
- [ ] _____
- [ ] _____
- [ ] _____
- [ ] _____
- [ ] _____
- [ ] _____
- [ ] _____
- [ ] _____

My Thoughts

Number Of Invitations	Cost Per Invitation	Cost Per Response Card	Cost Per Thank You	Estimated Total Cost	Number Of Programs	Cost Per Program	Estimated Total Cost	Number Of Placecards	Cost Per Placecard	Estimated Total Cost

Number Of	Cost Per	Cost Per	Cost Per	Estimated Total Cost	Number Of	Cost Per	Estimated Total Cost	Number Of	Cost Per	Estimated Total Cost

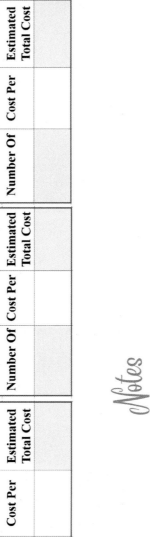

Notes

Bridal Shower

Bridal Shower

I know, I know, this is something that you typically will not be putting together and someone else will be in charge of coordinating this party. The reason we add it here is so you can create some boundaries and have some idea of what to expect. The last thing you want is Cousin Mae fighting with a bridesmaid about what they want it to look like and who will be invited. This will be great information for whoever puts on your Bridal Shower. Share it with them!

What To Ask Yourselves

- Do we want to have one?
- Who should be invited?
- When are we going to have it?
- Who will plan it?
- Who will be paying for it?
- What is the budget?
- Where will it be hosted?
- Is our photographer going to attend and capture the moment?
- What games will be played?
- What food and drinks will be served?
- Will it be casual or formal?
- Should there be a theme?
- What will the itinerary be?

Things You Haven't Thought About

- Brainstorm Session With The Bride
- Food & Drinks
- Games
- Gifts
- Slide Shows
- Time For Stories
- Decor

♥ Playlists
♥ Itinerary

Tips & Tricks

♥ Decide on a budget and stick to it.
♥ Make sure the date is ok with the bride before moving forward.
♥ This isn't your bachelorette party. Close female family & friends are welcome.
♥ The bridal shower is typically thrown 2 weeks to 3 months before the wedding.
♥ You might have more than one as co-workers seem to always be up for a good party (even if they know they might not be invited to the wedding).
♥ A close relative, maid of honor or bridesmaid will usually throw the bridal shower. The Mother or Mother In Law should not throw the party or host it.
♥ Your playlist should be energetic and cross generational.
♥ Party favors for the guests are a special touch.
♥ A standard itinerary for a bridal party would include setup, bride arrival, guest arrival, meal/bites, games, opening of gifts, toast to the bride, groom arrives, guests leave and finally clean up.
♥ The bridal shower is anywhere from two to four hours.
♥ Couple showers are becoming more trendy. Do you want to have a ladies only shower or a couples shower?
♥ There is a lovely tradition of taking the ribbons from all of the gifts from the bridal shower, making a bouquet out of them and using it as a stand-in at the wedding rehearsal. Does this sound like something you want to do? Tell the host.
♥ Gifts will take time to open. Plan accordingly.
♥ Most bridal showers are informal. DIY decorations, potlucks or small bites and homemade games at someone's home is OK if on a tight budget.

Insider Secrets

♥ Just because someone is hosting doesn't mean they have to do everything themselves. Recruit help!
♥ Send invites 4-6 weeks from the date you choose.
♥ Gifts given at the bridal shower are typically for your future home. Think

about what this might mean to you if you do a registry or wish list for it.

- The groom-to-be should show up near the end of the Bridal Shower (and usually with flowers for the bride to be).
- Inviting people to the shower who are not invited to the wedding is a no no. The exception would be if co-workers throw one for you.
- Set up an area for gifts.
- The host should toast the bride at some point during the party.
- Having a tripod for photos is more important than a seating chart for the shower.
- You may be working out like crazy for the wedding day, try to make special parties like the bridal shower a cheat day. Enjoy yourself to the fullest.
- Pass out desert while the gifts are being opened as this might be the longest portion of your itinerary.

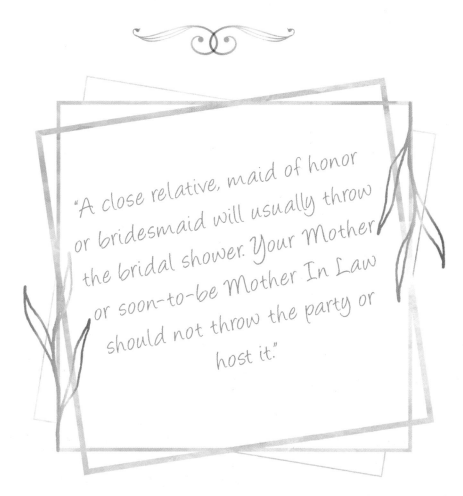

"A close relative, maid of honor or bridesmaid will usually throw the bridal shower. Your Mother or soon-to-be Mother In Law should not throw the party or host it."

Bridal Shower - To Do List

☐ _____
☐ _____
☐ _____
☐ _____
☐ _____
☐ _____
☐ _____
☐ _____
☐ _____
☐ _____
☐ _____
☐ _____
☐ _____
☐ _____
☐ _____
☐ _____
☐ _____
☐ _____

My Thoughts

Photographer
Videographer

Photographer Videographer

One of the best ideas that we have heard, and more than one time, is how a photographer or even a videographer can be used for an engagement session right after some beautification trials. Brides really hit their stride in planning when they have their hair and makeup trials done and, later on, benefit from the pampering and fantastic look for their engagement photos or video. You can even take it up a notch by having your engagement party after the photo session! Arrive in style!! Oh yeah, don't forget to have a backup of all of the engagement and wedding photos . . . and then backup the backup.

What To Ask A Photographer

- Will you be the one shooting my wedding?
- Can I meet the team that will be shooting my wedding?
- Will you have assistants or second shooters helping you that day?
- What will you and your assistants wear to the wedding?
- Do you also do videography?
- Do you have some recent weddings that we can see full galleries of?
- Can we request specific shots and if so when do we need to provide that list to you?
- Can we customize a package at my budget's price point?
- Are engagement photos, rehearsal dinners and other pre-wedding events included?

- Do you have a photobooth?
- Do you offer prints, albums and canvases? If so, what do they look like? How are the album photos chosen? What is the turnaround time?
- Will we have access and rights to all of the photos taken, even the ones you don't like?
- Do you have recommendations for other standout vendors that you have worked with? Have you worked with _____ (your already booked vendors) before?
- How would you describe your photography style?
- What is it like to work with you on our wedding day? Could you walk us through it?
- Do you offer certain styles of post-production or editing?
- Do you specialize in outdoor or indoor events?
- Do you ask for consent before sharing our wedding photos on social media, blogs, websites or magazines?
- How many hours are included?
- Do you have travel fees?
- Do you carry backup equipment?
- Are there things that aren't included that I should consider?
- What are the next steps?
- Do you have any references?

What To Ask A Videographer

- How many weddings do you film a year?
- How would you describe your video style?
- What things would you want from us to help you create a wedding video?
- How do you choose music for your videos?
- How do you get the audio for vows & speeches?
- Why did you choose filming weddings as a profession?
- Do you do this full or part time?
- Do you stage shots?
- How many hours are included?
- Could you tell me about your packages & can we custom create a package?
- How does your editing process work?
- Are you open to feedback for edits via a rough cut?
- Are there any vendors that you love to work with?
- Have you worked with any of our vendors before?

- Will you coordinate with my photographer?
- Will you need to connect to my DJ's soundboard to capture audio?
- Can we see some wedding videos that you have created?
- What do you and your assistants wear at the wedding?
- Do you use drones?
- Do you offer 4K or HD videos?
- Do you offer social media friendly excerpts? These can't have licensed music, so that one Sabrina Claudio song you both like can't be used on social media without it getting flagged.
- Do you create multiple backups of the footage just in case?
- How long after the wedding do you typically hand over the finished product?
- How will the video be delivered?
- What is your contingency for inclement weather?
- Who owns the rights to our video?
- Do you carry backup equipment?

Things You Haven't Thought About

- Engagement Photos/Videos
- Rehearsal dinner photos
- Albums/Prints
- Raw photo batches
- Guarantees. Ask about them and get it in writing.
- Practicing poses
- Your family & bridal party won't know that they have to be where they have to be for photos. Let them all know ahead of time, not the day of the wedding.
- Drone Usage
- Wedding invitation videos
- Hashtags for the wedding day (social media)
- Send video thank you notes

Tips & Tricks

- Make sure that you get along really well with your photographer and/or videographer. You will find out that they will be spending more time with you than most of your guests during the ceremony & wedding. Even if the person has the most beautiful photos and videos on the planet, if their style or communication annoys you, that will be a problem.

- Want more photos and videos from different perspectives? Set up your own hashtag before the wedding for social media. Then search the hashtag and get the photos and videos you love from those that attended.
- Create a facebook group to let guests share videos. There are apps that will let your guests upload videos & photos too.
- Practice your poses ahead of time, they'll be a bit more polished and you won't have someone walking over to you to tilt your head up and place your hands on your hips. Have a pose off . . . you versus the mirror.
- Make sure the groom is confident with being photographed. Have a photo shoot where each of you takes turns to become more comfortable with the shot.
- For staged photos, many people won't know what to do with their arms or hands. A good photographer will suggest what to do so the shot isn't awkward.
- Take phones out of your pockets for photos. Nobody wants to see any type of bulge!
- Make sure the photographer/videographer scouts out the venues before the wedding. This allows them to be familiar with potential photographic gems.
- If it's a sunny day for your wedding, a lot of people might have sunglasses on. Is this OK? If not, you may want to let your photographer know so she can direct people during group shots. Candid shots may not be so easy.
- Try to avoid food being served or eaten during the speeches. It makes for significantly better candid shots of people laughing and crying (in a good way).
- You need to have a good, long smooch for your first kiss for a great photo.
- Look at eachother, not the officiant during the ceremony. This will provide better angles (aka not the back of your heads) for photographs & video.
- Organizing tipsy people is very difficult. Be kind to your photographer and tell your bridal party to make sure they are listening to and assisting the photographer when asked.
- Let your photographer know about any unique details, special times or cultural highlights that they might not know about before the wedding. This allows them to prepare and not miss the traditions that they may have never seen or heard of before.
- Have you ever thought about asking your photographer about ceremony or reception layouts? They may know a thing or two plus have a great eye combined with their experience to offer fantastic ideas.
- An engagement photo shoot is a great test run to make sure you truly click

with your photographer.

- If potential photographers talk more about package, pricing & policies rather than you, your wedding and the day . . . you may want to move on.

- Shoot & Burn photography is usually pretty cheap. It's where the photographer takes all of the typical photographs they would normally take, but then simply moves the entire lot to a thumb drive or cloud link for you to do as you please with. No editing. No removing of the photos you or the photographer might not like.

- If you are planning on having a destination wedding, you may want more than just one day of photographs.

- If a pose or position is uncomfortable or awkward to you, skip it. Being uncomfortable will show up in the photo.

- Make sure you know the photo restrictions for your ceremony venue especially if it is a church. Father Michael might not like your photographer leaning against Mother Mary to get the right angle.

- Be adventurous with your locations and creative with your props.

- Don't forget to include some black and white photography when printing.

- Photographers are artists. They don't really want to copy all of the pictures you provided as examples. Instead ask them to add their own style while capturing a photo similar to what you want.

- Photos of you drunk will look different from photos when you are sober. Keep that in mind before you start slamming shots with the squad.

- Formal pictures should take place early on. Before that glass of Pinot Noir gets tipped just a little bit too much while taking a sip and ends up on the wedding dress.

- If you have a videographer, think about recording an interview talking about your love story. Do this before the wedding.

- Decide what key elements your videographer should capture. Their ability to capture moments may be significantly less than a photographer if there is only one person filming.

- If you are thinking about DIYing your videography make sure you designate one person to do so. Maybe even choose one friend for the ceremony and one for the reception. A tripod would be a good investment here.

- Speaking of DIY, if you livestream your wedding on Facebook you can save the video and have it edited after the fact.

- For DIY videography, find a camera that can hold a very large memory capacity by way of external storage like a microSD and record the event from beginning to end, only switching angles. This way you don't miss a thing if something happens too early or late when you've stopped the

recording because the timeline said nothing was going on for 30 minutes.
- The video you have can be an anniversary tradition to watch.
- A lot of video effects is a way for the videographer to show all their tricks of the trade but do you want it to feel cluttered and take away from the feel of the event you created? Make sure your wedding video is simple.
- Create your own photo booth.

Insider Secrets

- Most photographers won't say this outloud, but a few polaroid cameras and a selfie kit or two will be just as big of a hit as the add-on photo booth.
- Find a photographer that will give you all of the pictures taken on that day. Possibly on a thumb drive. This way you can find your most favorite photos and less expensive printing/album options to create your own prints. Plus, you'll be able to email photos to your friends or use them for the thank you cards.
- A receiving line with a twist! Have your photographer set up an area near the entrance or have a person greeting and directing people to a picturesque area of the venue. This is where you will be waiting as a couple, greet the guests and take a photo with them before they enter the main reception area. You will have the opportunity to greet and thank your guests, have a memory with them via a photo and won't be pressed to run around and speak to everyone during the reception.
- People are addicted to taking pictures with their phones, especially during key moments in the ceremony and reception. If you don't want your professional photos to have a background of a bunch of people holding up their cell phones, have a very visible & kind sign asking guests to unplug and enjoy the moment.
- Get ready for your wedding in an uncluttered room with a lot of natural light.
- You don't really need EVERY photo taken that night. So you want the photo of you with one eye closed and mouth open eating a lambchop pop or the shot of Great Grandma Pearl with the fly that landed on her plate?
- Yes, anything from 4-12 weeks is a possible turn-around time depending on the quantity and complexity of photos that need to be sorted, edited, reviewed and placed in albums or on canvases.
- If your special day straddles both day and night time make sure your

portrait time is split up between the two as well.

♥ If there is a potential for family drama or if there is family drama, let the photographer know. Cousin Shelly will be an instant Karen and make a scene if she is asked to take a picture with her ex Gary who is now in a serious relationship with cousin Charlie.

♥ Ask to see longer video edits from videographers you are considering. Not the short videos on their websites or social media. Long edits.

♥ Kindly ask your officiant ahead of time to step out of the frame for your first kiss.

"Look at eachother, not the officiant during the ceremony. This will provide better angles (aka not the back of your heads) for photographs & video."

Photographer/Videographer - To Do List

- [ ] _____
- [ ] _____
- [ ] _____
- [ ] _____
- [ ] _____
- [ ] _____
- [ ] _____
- [ ] _____
- [ ] _____
- [ ] _____
- [ ] _____
- [ ] _____
- [ ] _____
- [ ] _____
- [ ] _____
- [ ] _____
- [ ] _____
- [ ] _____
- [ ] _____

My Thoughts

Photographer Videographer	Contact Name	Phone	Email	Wedding Day Cost	Number Of Hours	Eng. Photo/Vid Cost	Photo/Video Album Cost	Total Estimated Cost	Notes

Notes

Honeymoon

Honeymoon

The key to a great honeymoon is to go to a place that checks off the top 3 things you want to do (beaches, art, mountains, seclusion, big city, etc.) in a location that you both can agree on. When Adam & I were thinking of honeymoon destinations, we each listed our top three activities and top three countries. From our list, we both had great food and beautiful beaches. We also had Italy in our top three destinations. Now picture this. It's a bright sunny day in Sorrento. A newly married couple decide to go to the Blue Grotto off of the Island of Capri. They move from the main boat onto a row boat with another couple, the four of them watch the opening of the grotto open and close with the movement of the ocean. They make it inside to see the Blue Grotto lit up in marvelous shades of blue. The other couple in the boat, in a thick Italian accent, reveal that they are a professional opera singer and conductor and ask if it is OK if they sing. The couple then are treated to 15 minutes of operatic loveliness as if it was their own personal concert. Yes, that happened to us!

What To Ask Yourselves

♥ When do we want to go?
♥ How long do we want our honeymoon to be?
♥ What do we want to do (relax, adventure, touristy things or a little bit of everything)?

- Domestic or Foreign Travel?
- Planes, Trains, Boats or Automobiles?
- Do we want two of our days consumed by flying and possibly a jetlag day or two?
- What level of accommodations do we want?
- Hotel, Resort or AirBnB?
- Will we both enjoy this destination?
- Do we have experience traveling to the area we are considering?
- Do we want privacy or be in the middle of the action?
- Is this the best time to visit this destination?
- What is the weather like for our scheduled dates?
- What do we need to pack?
- What are each of our top 3 things that we want to do in the area we are considering?
- Are our passports valid?

Things You Haven't Thought About

- Domestic travel vs foreign travel
- Staycation
- One long honeymoon or two shorter ones
- Last minute deals vs planned in advance
- Honeymoon cruises
- Asking guests to contribute to the honeymoon instead of getting three wine glass sets
- Passports
- Packing before the wedding
- Excursions
- Couples packages
- Mini-Moons & Multi-Moons

Tips & Tricks

- If you are using a Travel Agent check recent reviews, find out how long they have been doing it. Ask why they recommend certain destinations. Ask how they are paid (commission) and if they need a deposit as well as when the balance would be due.
- When planning the budget, think of every single expense that there will be including currency conversion fees, international credit card or ATM usage,

- travel taxes, insurance, resort fees, transportation fees, fun money & more.
- Really want to save money? How about a staycation?
- Sometimes "killer deals" on resorts are there for a reason. Check the latest reviews on anything you plan to book.
- Consider a cruise. This could cut your honeymoon costs in half.
- Don't copy your BFF's honeymoon or have relatives plan your honeymoon for you.
- We find that a combination of relaxation, adventure, exploration & tourism is the best way to go. Mix it up. Don't just lay on the beach for 10 days, or if you do, try different drinks at least.
- Stay within your abilities. We know that doing new and exciting things are part of the fun, but consider what you can and can't do. Don't book snorkeling if you barely know how to swim & don't plan a hike in the Alps if you haven't seen a treadmill or stair climber in 8 months.
- Don't overdo your trip. Planning an adventure, sight seeing far away from your hotel or an excursion every single day may wear you out. Have lazy & in love days planned throughout your trip.
- Have you heard of mini-moons (a short honeymoon trip) & multi-moons (multiple short trips throughout the first year of marriage)? Is this something you would consider outside of the big honeymoon?
- Add a surprise or two. This could come in the form of a special dinner in a secluded area of a restaurant. A gift hidden in your partner's luggage. A surprise excursion or something your sweetheart would love to do.
- Ask friends or family if they have been to the destinations you are choosing from. Make sure the people you ask match closely to what you like to do as a couple. Google, Travelocity, Friends/Family & Travel Professionals are your go-to for figuring out the best places for your getaway.
- Exchange your currency before you leave and check with your banks, as you notify them of your travel, whether there are additional charges for international ATM withdrawals or purchases.
- If you are planning on bringing a bunch of gifts and memories home with you, stay about 10 pounds under the baggage weight limit when departing for the honeymoon.
- Don't forget to have a small backpack with you for the trip. This will save you during day trips and exploring.
- Always have a phone or camera at the ready for those unexpected moments during the honeymoon. When Lucy & I were headed to the Blue Grotto, we seriously considered putting away the camera and leaving it on the main boat. What a mistake that would have been!

- Consider paying more for direct flights. Sometimes the extra hours you save is more beneficial than the extra money you will have to pay. Especially if you have a long flight and will need time to rest upon arrival.
- Take at least one portion of your trip (if not all) to splurge on where you are staying. One night in an upgraded suite can be a special and unexpected surprise.
- Ask your hotel or excursion company what the most romantic package that they offer is. Not only will you hear some things that may not be on their website, you may actually get a free upgrade or bonus amenity because it is your honeymoon.
- Couples Spa treatment. Your sweetheart probably has never been pampered at the level that is offered and you deserve it.

Insider Secrets

- Start planning your honeymoon early. You don't want all of the wedding planning to get in the way of your first special adventure that the two of you are taking as a married couple.
- Don't be afraid to ask for cash in lieu of gifts for your wedding. Say it is a tradition. Even if it isn't, it will become one once you start it. This cash can help pay for some credit cards you may have used for the wedding, pay for your honeymoon and give you some spending money for your honeymoon. From personal experience . . . best . . . thing . . . ever!
- There are honeymoon contribution sites out there, but make sure you read the fine print before utilizing one. You may end up giving a pretty decent percentage of the honeymoon funding to them. Imagine what that 3-7% fee would allow you to do on your honeymoon. Snorkeling day trip anyone?
- The best way to compromise on a honeymoon (you are two different people after all) is to write down your top 5 destinations as well as the top 3 things you want your honeymoon to be like. Reveal it to each other to see what you have in common and build from there. An example would be: Places- Jamaica, St. Lucia, Hawaii, Amalfi Coast & Spain. Wants- beautiful beaches, historical destinations & great food.
- Looking for less tourists than Hawaii or Paris has to offer? Try some less traveled to destinations like Guadeloupe, A Castle In Scotland, Zanzibar, Algarve, Alaska, Vietnam, Sri Lanka or Seychelles to name a few.
- If you don't have enough funds to cover a trip to where you want to go, place what you have in a separate account and have that account be a

sinking fund for your honeymoon. Once you have enough to cover the entire trip and all of the expenses plus spending money, book the trip. A honeymoon on your 1 year anniversary is still your honeymoon.

- Hopefully you know your partner's travel habits. Do they stress out planning them, packing for them, flying or when they are in new environments? Try to make these as comfortable and stress free as possible for them so that your honeymoon begins on a smooth note.

- Tell every place that you are booking with, in advance, that it is your honeymoon. Email them your story and why you are excited to go there. They may upgrade you. Tell everyone that you encounter at restaurants, museums or excursions that this is your honeymoon. This trip is special and you deserve to celebrate it in style. You'd be surprised at the extra special treatment you will receive simply by mentioning it.

- Directly confirm all of your reservations. All of them.

- Book under the maiden name if leaving shortly after the wedding. In all likelihood you haven't submitted for the name change.

- Get to the airport early. You know what is worse than hanging out at an airport? Rushing to the airport and stressing out whether you are going to make it in time. See Home Alone for the running to the gate visual example.

- There are many ways to get travel upgrades outside of letting people know the trip is for your honeymoon or by simply asking if they offer upgrades. Upgrades will be more likely if: you travel off season, some airlines allow you to bid on upgrades, checking into the hotel after the check in time which allows them to see what is available, traveling on a day where business travelers are least likely to travel like Saturdays, brand new hotels or resorts may be more inclined to offer upgrades OR you may have loyalty rewards/points that allow for upgrades.

Honeymoon - To Do List

- [ ] _____
- [ ] _____
- [ ] _____
- [ ] _____
- [ ] _____
- [ ] _____
- [ ] _____
- [ ] _____
- [ ] _____
- [ ] _____
- [ ] _____
- [ ] _____
- [ ] _____
- [ ] _____
- [ ] _____
- [ ] _____
- [ ] _____
- [ ] _____

My Thoughts

Destination	Excursion 1	Excursion 2	Estimated Spending Money	Estimated Flight Cost	Estimated Hotel Costs	Estimated Excursion Costs	Estiated Transportation Costs	Total Estimated Cost	Notes

Notes

Dresses
Tuxedos
Attire

Dresses | Tuxedos | Attire

I love Lucy! She definitely had some 'splaining to do when she told me how many dresses she was going to wear during the wedding and reception. Do you know how much fun it is to tell people she wore a dress every 30 minutes? I mean, it's not true but it's really fun. I think I add a dress every anniversary. She, of course, had her wedding dress. She had a traditional Ao Dai. She had a dress for the bouquet toss. Last, but not least, she had a cake cutting and dancing dress for when the night really kicked into gear.

What To Ask A Dress Maker

- Do I need to make an appointment and how much time should we block out for the appointment?
- How many people can I bring with me?
- Does my wedding date affect any possibilities with dresses?
- Do you have an in house seamstress?
- Do you have sample shoes to wear during my fitting or should I bring my own?
- If you don't have the dress I like in your salon, can I request a sample gown?
- Can I take photos of the dresses I like in your store?
- Are alterations included in the dress price?
- What is the cost for alterations?
- How many fittings will I have?
- Do you have any special shows coming up?
- How is your store different from others?
- What style do you think will enhance my body type?
- Is this dress customizable? What would the limitations be?
- Is it possible to buy a sample dress?

- What would your suggestions be for under the dress (certain dresses need certain undergarments)?
- Is there anything I should know about this dress?
- What accessories would you recommend for this dress?
- What happens if I change my mind?
- Do you store the dress for me until right before my wedding date?
- Will the dress be steamed right before pickup?
- How would you recommend I transport the dress?
- When is my final decision needed?
- What bridesmaids styles would compliment this dress?
- When should everyone have their measurements in by?
- What if my bridesmaids aren't local?
- What do you suggest for preserving my dress?
- What is your return policy?

What To Ask At A Men's Formal Wear Shop

- Do I need an appointment and how much time should I block off for the appointment?
- How many people can I bring to the appointment?
- What sets you apart from other formal wear shops?
- Is it possible to customize my suit/tux?
- What is the timeframe to order, get in and then tailor my suit/tux?
- How far in advance should I start looking for my suit/tuxedo?
- Are alterations included with the price of the suit/tux?
- How much do alterations cost?
- What accessories do you recommend for this suit/tux and do you carry them in stock?
- What style of groomsmen suits/tuxedos will complement this one?
- What if my groomsmen aren't local?
- When should everyone have their measurements in by?
- What is your return policy?

Things You Haven't Thought About

- Engagement party outfit
- Engagement photos outfit
- Bridal shower outfit
- Bachelor/Bachelorette party outfits

- ♥ Rehearsal dinner outfit
- ♥ Alterations of wedding dress/suit/tux
- ♥ Wedding shoes
- ♥ Reception outfit
- ♥ Next day brunch outfit
- ♥ Wedding dress preservation & cleaning
- ♥ Remember the climate for when you are getting married, not when you are trying your dress, suit or tuxedo on.
- ♥ Sit, stand and dance in the clothes you are thinking of buying. You will be doing all of these things. Have a song you know will get you moving ready on your phone.

Tips & Tricks

- ♥ If you want to save money, stay away from designer labels.
- ♥ Don't skimp on tailoring. Get the best fitting outfit you can. Close enough isn't the way to go here.
- ♥ Borrow outfits from your most stylish friends.
- ♥ Buy low cost shoes and bedazzle them yourself.
- ♥ Surprise your sweetheart with a custom liner that has pictures of memories as a couple for the suit or tux. If you are getting it for yourself, it could be a second "reveal" photo that will blow your love's mind.
- ♥ If your wedding is not in your city and you are traveling elsewhere for your wedding, don't ship your dress, tux or suit. Pack it in your bags and have it steamed once you get there. The last thing you want is a missing package... the package with your dress in it.
- ♥ There are styling services that will do everything from dressing the bride to steaming all of the garments. They'll also keep the groom & groomsmen looking sharp too!
- ♥ YOUR PHONES!!!! Inside jacket pockets for gents, purses or clutches for ladies. Better yet, have everyone check them in with your reception team so everyone can enjoy an evening disconnected from the Matrix. Imagine how many photos you'll have to disregard with people in the background staring at their phones. Trust us! It will be more than you think.
- ♥ Unlike the bride, you can get more than one use out of a suit or tuxedo. If you are choosing a suit, you will wear it significantly more than a tuxedo, however, a tuxedo will never go out of style and you can still use it for many other events... or to dress up like James Bond for a themed date night.

- For your tux or suit, you can never go wrong with a white button up.
- For tux/suit accessories, you may want to go with a tie or a bowtie and you most certainly would want to dress it up with a pocket square.
- If you are having a hard time deciding between a suit or a tuxedo, think about the ambiance of the wedding and how formal it is going to be. If you are going for a super elegant in the city look, you may want to opt for tux. If you are doing a more rural vineyard feel, then a suit may go best.
- Have you thought about matching socks for the groom and groomsmen? Make a statement with them!
- Lucy wore 15 dresses on our wedding night. OK, maybe only 5. This may be something you might do too so don't forget to add it to your budget along with the clothing for the engagement photos, engagement party, traditional cultural parties, bachelor & bachelorette parties and any other events leading up to the wedding like the rehearsal dinner.
- Don't bring all of the bridesmaids or groomsmen to your first appointment. The fewer "ideas" provided to you, the better.
- After you have bought your dress, stop shopping for dresses! This is the path that leads to self doubt and regret. Your choice was the right one. Go with it. Forget everything else.
- What you are wearing is for you. Buy what you want to see on yourself, not anyone else. Don't choose something someone else wants to see you in (except maybe your sweetheart).
- The style of your dress should not only fit your silhouette but also be a fancier version of your everyday style and personality.
- Take a photo or three in each dress and before you take it off, take a look at the photos. You want to see what you look like in photographs before saying yes to the dress.
- Eat before you shop and make sure you are in a positive "yes" type of mood. You don't want to be a hangry negative nancy which might make the perfect dress slip through your fingers because of mindset not because of the dress.
- Don't judge a potential dress on the hanger. Try it on first.

Insider Secrets

- Did you know that you could get up to half off and sometimes more for a gently used designer wedding dress that the shop used for display and try-ons?

- You will forget how the seamstress or dress specialist told you how your dress should lay when you are standing during your ceremony. Neither will your bridesmaids. Ask a friend to take a video of the instructions during your fitting.
- Bring comfortable shoes. You may want to ditch the heels and opt for chucks when hitting the dance floor.
- For ladies & gents, please, please oh please break in your shoes well before the wedding. Especially if you like to get your groove on and don't plan on switching them out for bedazzled kicks.
- Did you know that your tailor might be able to stitch the lining of your suit/tux pocket and button holes with thread that matches the color of the wedding?
- If you show up with a pinterest board with dresses from celebrity weddings or suits & tuxedo ensembles from the Grammys, know that your budget probably won't cover the designer look. You'd be surprised at how many guys go into a formal wear shop with that picture and tell the stylist the budget is $200.
- It could take 4-6 months for your dress to ship and another 6-8 weeks for special alterations. Keep this in mind for the best shopping experience.
- Most wedding dress appointments take an hour and a half. Try not to book more than 3 in one day and make sure they are spaced out for food and travel time in between.
- Weekday mornings are substantially less busy than weekend afternoons. You also will have more attention from the specialist you are working with as well.
- State your mind. The last thing anyone wants is a timid bride or groom trying things on they don't like at all but are afraid to speak up. You won't hurt any feelings and your opinion will guide the stylist towards the perfect selection. That doesn't mean be closed minded, the perfect dress or suit might just be one you never thought about before.
- For the clothing that you wear on your wedding day, you should go with your heart more than your head. Your heart will sync up to the emotions you have that day. A checklist in your head of details you want will not convey to the day.
- Some salons and formal wear shops will bundle together the dress, veil and accessories and the suit, tie, shoes, belt, suspenders, socks and pocket square.
- Wear a little bit more makeup than usual for wedding dress shopping. It will make you feel a bit more special than usual and you will be able to imagine your special day that much more.

- Yes, your dress stylist might see you naked when trying wedding dresses on as they will be assisting you when taking delicate materials on and off. A strapless bra, boy shorts and the size heel shoe you are planning on wearing are recommended.
- We know, we know. Everyone plans on losing weight before the wedding. Few are good at it, most are where they are because their lifestyle isn't changing drastically in the next 12 months. Shop for how your body looks right now (which is beautiful) not what you plan your body to look like in the future (which is beautiful too). It is easier to take dresses in than it is to let them out when doing alterations.

"Take a photo or three in each dress and before you take it off, take a look at the photos. You want to see what you look like in photographs before saying yes to the dress."

Dresses/Tuxedos - To Do List

- [ ] _____
- [ ] _____
- [ ] _____
- [ ] _____
- [ ] _____
- [ ] _____
- [ ] _____
- [ ] _____
- [ ] _____
- [ ] _____
- [ ] _____
- [ ] _____
- [ ] _____
- [ ] _____
- [ ] _____
- [ ] _____
- [ ] _____
- [ ] _____

My Thoughts

Business	Contact Name	Phone	Email	Alteration Cost	Dress Cost	Suit/Tux Cost	Other Clothing Costs	Total Estimated Cost	Notes

Notes

MakeUp
Hair
Lashes
Beauty

MakeUp | Hair | Lashes | Beauty

From experience I can tell you two things. Don't wait for the last minute and always have a backup plan. Having been in the beauty industry for close to a decade now, I have seen many different reactions and mishaps from all of the beautification you will be doing for your wedding. When I was getting married I waited to dye my hair until the week of the wedding. On my wedding day, early in the morning, my stylist and I noticed that my hair had a green tone to it. I actually had to re-tone my hair the morning of my special day and it contributed to me almost being late to my own wedding! That and my make-up artist was sick and couldn't make it so we had to call in the back up artist. The moral of the story is don't do beautification that will affect your look the week of. Try two weeks to a month out. Also, have a backup artist for hair & makeup just in case.

What To Ask A Make-Up Artist

- Do you specialize in wedding makeup?
- What is included in your bridal package?
- Do you travel to my venue?
- How long will makeup take on the day of the wedding?
- How many people are you able to accommodate on my wedding day?
- How long will you be staying on the wedding day?
- Do you do a makeup trial?
- How long does the makeup trial take?

- How do I prepare for the makeup trial and the wedding day?
- What brands of makeup do you use?
- Are there products that I will need to buy for the wedding day?
- Have you worked with brides with my skin tone before?
- Would you be open to using my own makeup?
- How should I prepare my skin leading up to the wedding?
- If I get a spray tan, how would it affect my makeup?
- If I have lash extensions, do you know what product to use around the eyes that won't conflict with the glue used to apply them?
- Do you do touch-ups throughout the day and if so is there an additional cost?
- When should I book by?

What To Ask A Hairstylist

- Do you specialize in wedding hair?
- What is included in your bridal package?
- Do you travel to my venue?
- How long will hair take on the day of the wedding?
- Will you also work with my bridal party?
- Do you offer hair extensions?
- What other services do you provide?
- Do you offer a trial day? How long will it take?
- Do you have a team of stylists?
- Do you bring your own products?
- What products do you use?
- Do you charge by the hour or by the person?
- When should I book by?

What To Ask A Lash Artist

- How far out should I have the lashes done?
- Can I try lashes out before my engagement photos so I know what to expect?
- What style of lashes would you recommend for my wedding?
- What is the pricing for the different styles of lashes?
- Would you recommend lash extensions or a lash lift?
- How long will your services take?
- When should I book by?
- How should I prepare before getting lashes done?

💜 What are the benefits of lash extensions or a lash lift?

Things You Haven't Thought About

💜 Waxing
💜 Facials
💜 Mani-Pedi
💜 Professional Shave
💜 Lash Lift
💜 Eyebrows
💜 Spray Tan
💜 Lash Extensions
💜 Teeth Whitening
💜 Wedding Party & Mom Hair/Makeup
💜 Gratuity

Tips & Tricks

💜 Go to the salon instead of having them come to you. Unless they give you a deal for mobile service and it happens to be the same price.
💜 Beauty always takes longer than expected no matter who is doing it. Give yourself about a 30 minute buffer between your beautification and the next thing on your day-of schedule.
💜 Hair & Makeup will take longer for each of your bridesmaids and Moms as well. If the artist tells you 30 minutes, add an additional 15 minutes to the schedule per person. The last thing you want is a frantic bridal party worried about other things because your 3 hours of hair turned into 4.
💜 Lash extensions are actually quite easy to care for and will enhance your makeup. As a matter of fact, you typically need less eye makeup when you have eyelash extensions.
💜 Do you think there might be the slightest possibility that you will cry before and during the wedding? Of course you will! Lash Extensions mean no runny mascara.
💜 Eyelash Extensions are applied one by one or in mini fans whereas Strip Lashes are one size fits all.
💜 Strip Lashes can look amazing, but will only last for one day. Lash Extensions can be maintained as long as you want and will be on for your honeymoon and all the pictures you take on that amazing adventure with your sweetheart.

- Getting your lashes done and maintaining them a month or more before the wedding means you will have stunning, flirty eyes for all of the events leading up to your day.
- If you've never had lashes done before, you may want to pay a little bit extra for an experienced artist (they may go by Senior or Master Lash Artist).
- Once you have lashes done, stay away from oil based products as they can have a negative effect on the glue that was used to apply the extensions.
- Avoid using new-to-you products the day of the wedding.
- If you are having the entire bridal party, the moms and the grandmas done up on your special day, keep in mind that your hair and makeup should be done close to last, but not last. This way you don't feel rushed if everyone else goes over. There are exceptions, like if you are having some specific photos done early. This is a very important detail for your day of timeline.
- Discuss who is paying for what early on in your wedding planning when it comes to beautification. If your bridal party wants professional hair and makeup done it is proper etiquette that they pay for it. If you want their hair and makeup professionally done, you should pay for it. At the very least they should be tipping the artists after being pampered.
- Get your haircut 3 weeks before the wedding which allows your hair a chance to settle. For color, do this around 5 to 6 weeks out.
- If you are planning on DIY makeup, you may want to opt for a friend to do it instead. You know that one friend whose makeup is always on point or does makeup tutorials on Tik-Tok?
- Simple always works. Don't overdue the makeup. You want to have a natural look that is slightly more involved than you typically would do yourself for a night out downtown. Your wedding day is not the time to experiment.
- Drink a lot of water before your wedding. Hydrated skin is happy skin.
- Your manicure, fake nails & polish should be simple with soft shades. Bright colors show off chips more and may distract from the dress as well as your beautiful rings in close up photos.
- Come in prepared with what you want done and focused on what is being done (not your phone) for your hair and makeup trials as well as on the day of your wedding.
- Take into consideration the season of when your wedding takes place. Will it be hot? Is it the rainy season? Snow? It matters.
- If you are doing your own hair and makeup or a friend/family member

is. Practice. A whole bunch.

- Also, if you are doing your own makeup make sure you know how to rock primers, perfectly matched creamy foundations, setting sprays, layered lip colors & other tips & tricks that are readily available on your favorite social media.
- Have you thought about changing your hairstyle between the ceremony & reception? Talk about next level!
- Bring a friend to the makeup & hair trial that you trust will give their honest opinion and who understands your style. A second opinion may help you with important decisions.
- Last minute additions of people you want styled is not a good thing for your stress levels or the stress levels of the stylists assisting you. Be clear to everyone that your day of timeline is set, tight and can't have additions.
- Natural & Matte finishes are essential for hot, summer weddings.
- For your trials, take a lot of photos from different angles and bring a notebook for notes so you can write down any preparation techniques suggested by your chosen professionals.
- Designate a beauty assistant to help you on your wedding day. Your beauty assistant should also make sure anything that you are using isn't used by someone else. Cross contamination is a real thing that you don't want to affect you on the big day.
- Make a list of beauty and health habits that will make you feel your best. This should be done around 12 months out.

Insider Secrets

- Schedule your makeup & hair trial on the day of your engagement photoshoot. Two for one!
- Bring Photos and be as specific as possible with what you want. Visual aids always will help a stylist.
- Nude lipstick won't translate well in photos. If you want your lips to stand out but not be overbearing. Go for red! Rose to be exact.
- Eyelash Extensions are not a certain amount of lashes to make a specific look. The lash professional will be able to look at your existing lashes and find ways to enhance it in a way that matches your style and the look of your overall wedding beautification.
- Book your eyelash extensions 2-4 weeks before the wedding with a refill booking a few days before your special day. There are different glues that can be used in case of an allergic reaction during your first visit & you'll

want to see if you have a reaction way before your wedding.

- 🤍 Your lash artist will give you preparation and maintenance tips for your lash extensions. Listen carefully and follow those instructions to get the most out of your new look.
- 🤍 Your lashes should last around 6 to 8 weeks. Refilling them every 2 to 3 weeks will keep the look up. If you want them removed, have it done by a lash artist. The last thing you want to do is pull off the lashes yourself because your natural lashes will go with them.
- 🤍 With more abrasive beautification such as eyebrows, waxing & other spa treatments, we suggest having them done 4-7 days or more out to avoid redness, reactions or soreness on the wedding day. This allows you time to correct any issues as well.
- 🤍 Have a fan available for ventilation and to cool you down during your beautification process the day of the wedding. Sweating is bad.
- 🤍 Expect an early start if you and your entire glam squad is having their hair and makeup done the day of.
- 🤍 Getting ready robes isn't just a way to look super cute with the team while getting ready. It's a way to make sure your wedding attire isn't stained when having your hair & makeup done. Get dressed last.
- 🤍 A daily vitamin with biotin beginning 4 months out will do wonders for your hair. You can also detox your hair 2 to 3 times before the wedding day.
- 🤍 A detoxifying facial combined with military-like discipline in a moisturizing regimen will assist in the application of your wedding day makeup and will allow for it to last longer.
- 🤍 Don't try any skin treatments you haven't done before the week of your wedding and preferably two weeks of the wedding. You may have an adverse reaction that will not be a good look.
- 🤍 Blotting papers. Have them in your touch up bag. It's a must.
- 🤍 If you have a separate room than the room that everyone else is getting ready in, make it the makeup and hair room where only the person being attended to will be in it. A quiet and peaceful place will not only help you, but the artists.
- 🤍 On your special day, pay attention to the makeup and hair throughout the process (including the back of your hair) so you can guide the stylist towards any changes you'd like to make.
- 🤍 Make sure you don't overwhelm your stylist with 37 pinterest ideas. Narrow down what you want to about 2 or 3 styles. Also, bring pictures of your wedding dress including whether or not you are going to wear a veil and tell them the style of wedding you are going to have.

- When going to your hair and makeup trials, try to wear a top that is the same shade as your dress. It makes a difference!
- After your trials for hair and makeup, wear it the entire rest of the day. You'll want to see how it all holds up.
- If you're going swimming after the wedding or during the honeymoon, rinse off your lashes with fresh water to reduce the chance of losing some.

"Beauty always takes longer than expected no matter who is doing it. Give yourself about a 30 minute buffer between your beautification and the next thing on your day-of schedule."

Beautification - To Do List

- [ ] _____
- [ ] _____
- [ ] _____
- [ ] _____
- [ ] _____
- [ ] _____
- [ ] _____
- [ ] _____
- [ ] _____
- [ ] _____
- [ ] _____
- [ ] _____
- [ ] _____
- [ ] _____
- [ ] _____
- [ ] _____
- [ ] _____
- [ ] _____

Beautification - To Do List

- [ ] _____
- [ ] _____
- [ ] _____
- [ ] _____
- [ ] _____
- [ ] _____
- [ ] _____
- [ ] _____
- [ ] _____
- [ ] _____
- [ ] _____
- [ ] _____
- [ ] _____
- [ ] _____
- [ ] _____
- [ ] _____
- [ ] _____
- [ ] _____
- [ ] _____

My Thoughts

Beauty Service	Contact Name	Phone	Email	Bride Cost	Groom Cost	Bridesmaid Cost	Mothers Cost	Total Estimated Cost	Notes

Notes

Florist

Florist

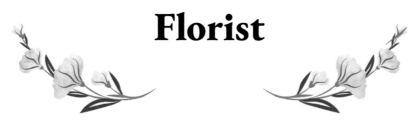

We've been asked many times before what our favorite floral experience was at a wedding and I must say, it's probably a tie between two weddings. One wedding was just full of flowers. Flowers everywhere! Not in an overwhelming way, but in a decorative and tasteful way. The bill for flowers alone must have matched the reception dinner. What could have tied it? Believe it or not it was a DIY floral setup where centerpieces, archways and accent flowers just seamlessly came together. You would have thought a professional spent half the day setting it up when in fact it was family members of the bride.

What To Ask A Florist

- Do you do the arrangements yourself?
- How far in advance do you create the arrangements & bouquets?
- How would you describe your style?
- Could you tell me about your process when you work with clients?
- Would you like to see styles that I like and would you be able to replicate those?
- Considering the season and my colors, what flowers would you recommend?
- Do you do a walkthrough of the venue beforehand?
- Could you work with my cake designer to provide flowers?
- Is there a minimum budget? What are your packages?
- Can I customize a package?
- Do you preserve bouquets after the wedding? If not, who do you recommend?
- Can you give me recommendations based on what I want but that can fit within my budget?
- What pieces do you provide with the flowers and what needs to be rented?
- Do you charge a delivery & setup fee?

- Do you breakdown as well and what is that fee?
- Will you move flowers from the ceremony site to the reception site?
- Is there an additional fee for a sample arrangement that I can see before signing a contract?
- How far in advance do I need to book you?
- When do you need the final numbers of the bridal party, parents/ grandparents and tables?

Things You Haven't Thought About

- A Toss Bouquet (different from your wedding bouquet)
- Corsages for mothers/grandmothers
- Flowers for the flower girl
- Petals for the flower girl
- Altar flowers
- Ceremony arch flowers
- Reception centerpieces
- Wedding cake flowers
- What is in season at the time of your wedding?
- Delivery fees
- Don't just think dollars, think scents. Powerful yet wonderfully smelling flowers at tables could actually change the way your meal tastes.
- Flowers that compliment not only your wedding color scheme but the wonderful colors of your meal aren't often thought of . . . but should be.

Tips & Tricks

- There may be a wholesale flower business near you. If so, you might find that you can get bulk flowers for less. You can then have a bridesmaids and family flower party to create the centerpieces and floral decorations the day before the wedding.
- After the ceremony. Have empty vases at the main tables for the bridesmaids to place their bouquets in. They now become decorative table pieces. Two for one!!!
- Instead of boutonnieres try matching pocket squares for all the gents in the wedding.
- If you have long tables, try alternating local fruits from a farmers market in bowls or tiered cupcake stands with your flowers. Half flowers, half edible centerpieces. Win, win.

- Ever hear of a floral pocket square? Google it. It's amazing!
- Check out local farmers markets for flowers. Talk to them about what it would look like to have them supply the flowers for your wedding.
- You may want to get a tossing bouquet instead of tossing the one you have used throughout your day. Do you really think Gertrude is going to let you pry the bouquet from her kung-fu grip after she dove across the dance floor so you can preserve it?
- Stay consistent with your color scheme.
- If you are going DIY keep it super simple. Also, try hybrid DIY. Do all of the table arrangements and floral decorations yourself but keep the bouquet and boutonnieres for the professionals.
- Staying on the DIY topic, blend in some non-floral accents and play it safe with a backup plan. Just in case.
- Have you ever heard of a wedding garden? Growing your own flowers for the wedding might be your kind of green thumb DIY.
- Talk to people you know about florists that they may have used in the past.
- You can cut costs by picking up your own flowers.

Insider Secrets

- In season and local flowers matter and will lower your expenses.
- The addition of inexpensive non-floral decorations accompanied with flowers will mean less money spent on flowers and more for other areas of your budget.
- Skip the flowers at the bar and on the isles at the ceremony. It will save you money and won't be missed.
- Outdoor weddings wreak havoc on flowers. Some are more resilient than others. If you are having an outdoor wedding during the summer, make sure your florist knows.
- Think about your venue & table arrangements before you make floral decisions.
- Some flowers have look-alikes that can save you money. Also, you can get an out of season look with an in season visual twin.
- Have you ever tried to have a conversation with a person standing between you and the person you're talking to? Well, if you have a huge arrangement in the middle of your table, this is what is going to happen to the people on opposite sides.
- Flower shops typically restock on Mondays.

Florist - To Do List

- [ ] _____
- [ ] _____
- [ ] _____
- [ ] _____
- [ ] _____
- [ ] _____
- [ ] _____
- [ ] _____
- [ ] _____
- [ ] _____
- [ ] _____
- [ ] _____
- [ ] _____
- [ ] _____
- [ ] _____
- [ ] _____
- [ ] _____
- [ ] _____
- [ ] _____

My Thoughts

Florist	Contact Name	Phone	Email	Bride Bouquet	Bridesmaid Bouquets	Boutineers	Decor Costs	Misc. Flower Costs	Total Estimated Cost	Notes

Notes

Entertainment

Entertainment

I'm putting this in the entertainment section because it is so fun and entertaining for your guests. You know the guestbook? How about an audio or video guestbook where your guests record a message to you for the wedding. What a great way to celebrate anniversaries! Each year you can look back and listen to or watch the messages. I've also seen typewriter guest books and quilt square guest books if you're thinking outside of the box.

What To Ask A DJ

- Will you be the one DJing our wedding?
- Tell me about your style.
- What are your favorite songs to play?
- Do you also do lighting?
- Are there other services that you provide that I might not know about?
- Can you emcee the event as well?
- How do you get the crowd dancing? What if that doesn't work?
- Do you have a recording of a recent wedding that we can watch to see you in action?
- If I'm having a hard time choosing songs for key moments, can you help me select them?
- Can you get any song? If I provide you a list, how will you incorporate other songs to fill the time?
- How many breaks do you need throughout the event?
- When do you usually take breaks?
- If we don't want guests making requests, how would you handle that?
- What are your rates and does this include from setup all the way through breakdown?

- How much time do you need for set up & sound check?
- What kind of space do you need?
- Do you provide sound and mics for the ceremony & reception (speeches, etc.)?
- How do you choose an appropriate sound level for guests of all ages?
- Do we need to rent any equipment or do you provide everything?
- What do you wear to weddings?
- When do we need to give you our song lists?
- What else do you need from us?

What To Ask A Band Or Musicians

- How long have you all been playing together?
- Will you be the one performing at my wedding? Will all the members of your band be there?
- If you or other band members aren't able to perform for one reason or another, what is the backup plan?
- What style of music do you play?
- What are your favorite songs to perform?
- Can you emcee the event as well?
- Do we need to rent any equipment or instruments or do you provide everything needed?
- How do you get the crowd dancing? What if that doesn't work?
- Do you have a recording of a previous wedding that shows your style?
- If I'm having a hard time choosing songs for key moments, can you help me select them?
- If I provide a song list, can you perform them or do you have a list to choose from?
- When do you usually take breaks?
- What are your rates & does this include set up to break down?
- How much time do you need for setup & sound check?
- What kind of space do you need?
- Do you provide sound and mics for the ceremony and reception (speeches, etc.)?
- How do you choose an appropriate sound level for guests of all ages?
- What do you all wear?
- When do we need to give you playlists?
- What else do you need from us?

Things You Haven't Thought About

♥ Sound Systems
♥ Microphones
♥ Ceremony entertainment vs reception entertainment
♥ Aside from DJs & Musicians you can have other entertainers at your wedding. Singing waiters, flash mobs, beatboxers, fire dancers, petting zoos… the sky's the limit . . . like a drone light show.
♥ We can keep going on and on about alternative entertainment ideas… sparklers, s'mores, cigar bars, bourbon bars, caricaturists, table trivia, mobile casino, giant jenga, celebrity look-alikes, slideshows & more.

Tips & Tricks

♥ Just as important as a playlist is the Do Not Play list. Songs you absolutely do not want to hear during the wedding. I mean, someone might like the soundtrack to Frozen but it might turn the dance floor cold.
♥ Ask the entertainment for an itinerary. If you have multiple entertainers, they will need to coordinate. Make sure they are open to do so.
♥ There are good DJs and good musicians out there, but the great ones become the wedding coordinator when it comes to the flow of the ceremony in some cases and most certainly the cocktail hour and wedding reception.
♥ Make sure there are enough power outlets for the equipment your entertainment is using. You don't want to short out the whole venue because there are 4 power strips daisy chained into 2 plugs in a 19th century building.
♥ Some venues do not allow bands. Make sure yours does if you want live entertainment outside of a DJ.

Insider Secrets

♥ Check with your venue to see if there are any noise ordinance, noise restrictions or complaints that they receive from neighbors that have been an issue before booking the venue.
♥ Shut down the "guest requests". Let your entertainment know that you'd like them to stick to the play list or similar. The last thing you want is Niki Menaj saying, well, Niki Minaj things. Great at the club. Maybe not

with grandma on the dance floor. She may hurt something!

- ♥ You may have a long list of songs that could probably fill the whole night, but there are certain songs that professionals know will get the crowd energy up. Let them have a bit of leeway.
- ♥ As the master of ceremonies the best DJs & Musicians are verbalizing in fun and creative ways what needs to be done or what is going on to garner the attention of the couple, guests and the wedding party.
- ♥ You can save money by hiring one entertainer whether that is a band or DJ to work both the ceremony and the reception even if they are in two different locations. For a band, perhaps the guitarist could play an acoustic guitar. Maybe the DJ can play all of the instrumental music you want played during the ceremony.

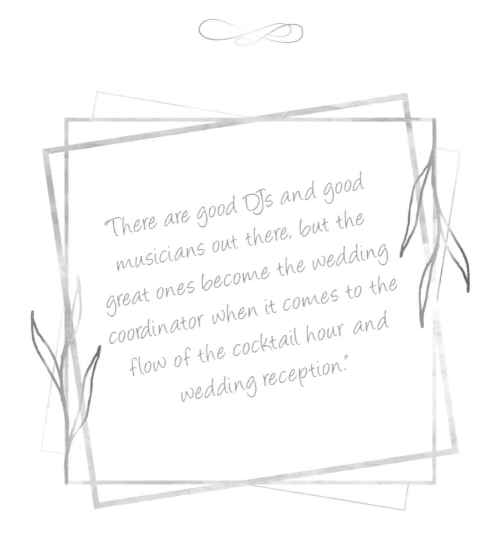

"There are good DJs and good musicians out there, but the great ones become the wedding coordinator when it comes to the flow of the cocktail hour and wedding reception."

Entertainment - To Do List

- [ ] _____
- [ ] _____
- [ ] _____
- [ ] _____
- [ ] _____
- [ ] _____
- [ ] _____
- [ ] _____
- [ ] _____
- [ ] _____
- [ ] _____
- [ ] _____
- [ ] _____
- [ ] _____
- [ ] _____
- [ ] _____
- [ ] _____
- [ ] _____

My Thoughts

Business	Contact Name	Phone	Email	Ceremony	Reception	Hours Included	Total Estimated Cost	Notes

Notes

Cake

Cake

We can't lie. We were caught up in the cupcake craze that hit weddings all across the country. Our wedding wasn't the first, and it wasn't the last, and we know this because we enjoyed cupcakes all along the way. Now, maybe it didn't take too much convincing because my Mom used to make cupcakes for the first day of school (all the way through the first year of college) and there was some nostalgia there. After all, it was going to be the first day of marriage. Oh yeah, our girls are getting cupcakes on their first days of school too!

What To Ask A Wedding Cake Baker

♥ What is your culinary background?
♥ When is the cake baked for the wedding?
♥ What flavors do you offer?
♥ What fillings do you offer?
♥ Do you specialize in a particular style or flavor of cake?
♥ How do you price your cakes?
♥ Is a tasting included, if not what is that cost?
♥ Do you do custom designs?
♥ Do you finish your cakes with fondant or buttercream?
♥ Do you work with florists to add flowers to the cake?
♥ How will the cake be displayed? Do you provide the displays or do you rent them?

- Do you provide a box for the top tier to be saved & frozen?
- Is there a delivery fee?
- How do you deliver the cake? What happens if it is damaged while being delivered?
- How are rented items returned?
- When do you suggest ordering the cake?
- When do you need the final guest count?

Things You Haven't Thought About

- Cake display
- Cake topper
- Cake cutting fee
- Cake cutting utensils
- Delivery fee
- Additional deserts (if you're doing a desert station)
- Preservation for 1 year anniversary

Tips & Tricks

- Find a wedding cake vendor that also does desert stations (2 for 1).
- Multiple smaller cakes may be more cost effective than a large cake for your wedding.
- Some bakers prepare the cake ahead of time and then freeze it before delivering. Make sure they bake it fresh for you if you don't want a possible frozen mishap.
- See if your cake artist offers other deserts that you may be interested in for a station or treats.
- An all white cake is always timeless.
- Order less slices than guests. Not everyone is going to eat cake. Usually 1 in 5 say thanks but no thanks.
- Negotiate your cake cutting fee. If the venue is doing it, negotiate it with them. Caterer? Same thing.
- Have you ever heard of a Groom's cake? It is a southern tradition where the groom can show his style and passion and is separate from the Bride's cake that is cut by the couple and served in the traditional way. The Groom's cake can be sliced for a late night snack or as a treat for guests to take home as they leave.
- Put some thought into your cake topper. This should be something that

represents the both of you or the theme/style of the wedding.

💜 Dummy tiers can cut costs if you want a grandiose cake.

Insider Secrets

💜 Purchase a two tier cake that is on display and that you cut into at the reception, but have sheet cake in the back that will be served to your guests. Make sure the cake is cut out of site after your first cut though.

💜 Buttercream over fondant, it saves you money.

💜 The inside flavor should match the outside flavor.

💜 Wedding style, decor and visions that you are going to do at your venue could be conveyed with your wedding cake as well. Let the professional cake baker and decorator know about it. They will more than likely have some great ideas.

💜 Don't want to use real flowers on your cake? Ask your baker if they do sugar flowers?

💜 By asking the slices of cake to be smaller, you will have more plates going out with less expensive cake needed.

💜 If you are having an outdoor wedding on a warm summer day, you may want to stay away from whipped cream, buttercream & meringue.

💜 One thing that many bakers who have delivered countless wedding cakes have seen is a cake table that is an afterthought. You should think about how this table will look and how it will be displayed & decorated so that it will flow with the style of the wedding and the cake.

💜 Have your wedding date, venue, style & estimated number of guests before you worry about your cake.

Cake - To Do List

- [ ] _____
- [ ] _____
- [ ] _____
- [ ] _____
- [ ] _____
- [ ] _____
- [ ] _____
- [ ] _____
- [ ] _____
- [ ] _____
- [ ] _____
- [ ] _____
- [ ] _____
- [ ] _____
- [ ] _____
- [ ] _____
- [ ] _____
- [ ] _____
- [ ] _____

My Thoughts

Bakery	Contact Name	Phone	Email	Cost Per Slice	Transport Cost	Sweets Table	Cake Table Cost	Total Estimated Cost	Notes

Notes

Seating Chart

Seating Chart

Oh, the seating chart. The glorious topic of much debate. While easy at first, it gets more complicated as you move away from the sweetheart table. Most weddings have the dance floor separating the sweetheart table or the wedding party table from the rest of the guests. We love the thought of an offset look with the couple slightly closer to the guests on one side where they can be placed near the closest family members. Good friends and younger family members that are not part of the wedding party can then be seated closest to the dance floor. As you work your way out you may choose to have friends and family that you don't see often and then co-workers as well as obligated invites near the back. No matter what you choose, just remember that next to nobody will become a Karen about their seating arrangement.

What To Ask Yourself

- How do we want the seating arrangement to be for the ceremony?
- What do we want the seating arrangements to look like at the reception?
- Who should be seated together?
- Should we mix guests or keep familiarity among the tables?
- What is the best flow for how the tables will be set up?
- Will we have a solo sweetheart table or have wedding party tables next to us?
- Are we going to assign every single seat for the reception?

Things You Haven't Thought About

♥ Ask for the venue floor plans that they use for weddings
♥ Shapes of the tables
♥ Seating for the ceremony
♥ Timing between a completed seating chart and printing materials
♥ Religious traditions for seating
♥ Guests with disabilities

Tips & Tricks

♥ Don't wait for all of the RSVPs. Make an ideal seating chart and make adjustments once all of the RSVPs are in or the deadline has approached.
♥ Seating charts should be completed with enough time to have all of the printed materials created like the escort cards, seating chart display, place cards & personalized menus.
♥ Stay away from the free-for-all seating arrangement for the reception. You don't want Uncle Charles wondering why nobody is sitting next to him or your high school age second cousin having flashbacks from elementary school lunch breaks of full tables and nowhere to sit.
♥ The ceremony site may have seating traditions, particularly if it is at a religious site, so ask the officiant or venue. The same goes for where the bride/groom sits or stands.
♥ It doesn't hurt to ask the parents which extended family members should sit with each other.
♥ Seating chart signage is essential if you don't want people wandering all about trying to figure out if their card matches the table they are supposed to sit at. Especially if the table signs aren't particularly large.
♥ VIPs should have the best view. Everyone else should be arranged by how they know the couple and how well they know the people at the tables around them.
♥ Have a kids table if there are enough to fill one (or more).
♥ A singles table might sound fun, but think of whether you have enough mutual friends at that table to make it more enjoyable. This isn't speed dating, it's a wedding.
♥ Guests with disabilities or elderly guests that might need more space to sit and stand should be placed with extra room at their table.
♥ If your sweetheart doesn't have a big family and you do, it may be better to eliminate a bride or groom's side for the ceremony. Do you really want a

packed left side and a sparse right side in the pictures? Have the usher seat the guests evenly in this case.

- Huh? What!?! Sorry for the garlic shrimp scampi breath while yelling two inches from your ear, but don't you think this speaker is a bit too close to our table? Totally digging the Frozen soundtrack though! Make sure you think about these things before you complete your floor plan.
- Remember the different priority lists from the invitation section? Utilize this to designate tables, with the people farthest from your must haves being seated the farthest from the couple's table, wedding party tables & parent tables.
- For guests that have small infants or guests that need wheelchair access, it would be beneficial to have them seated near the exits or restrooms for ease of access and in case a tantrum pops up at the most inopportune time.
- If you have a table or two where most people don't know each other, try seating them based on commonalities or assign a person from your wedding party to introduce them to one another mentioning their similar backgrounds.
- Picnic blankets, love seats, seats in circles, hay bales, arched seating, ottomans, pews & mismatched colorful chairs. Your ceremony doesn't have to go the traditional white chairs in balanced rows with an aisle in the middle route. Be you!
- During the ceremony the first five rows should be immediate and extended family as well as other VIPS.
- Have you thought about not having a sweetheart table at all? Leave two seats open at every table so you can spend time at each one. Your meal would be with the VIP table.
- Family Feud is an awesome game with some hilarious answers given at times, but it won't be so funny if you have two feuding individuals at the same table. Steve Harvey isn't going to meander on over to break the tension with a few one liners and his mesmerizing smile.

Insider Secrets

- Assign tables, not seats, unless you are having a very large wedding.
- If you are having trouble filling a table or two, use the Kevin Bacon strategy. Place one person who in one way or another happens to know all of the other people (who might not all know each other). That person will be the conversation starter and provide introductions if needed.

- Extra room at tables will help you at that perfect time when your good friend Ella brings a plus one when you weren't expecting it because she forgot to check the box on the RSVP. When you have an elbow to elbow table, you wouldn't be able to slide him in as you would with a table that has extra room.
- If you place the younger guests by the DJ they won't be deaf by the end of the night, get a headache from the loud music and are more likely to hit the dance floor to get the party started.
- Spacing between tables is important too. Guests should be able to push their chair back and still be able to walk around it without bumping into other guests at the next table.
- When creating the configuration of your tables, make sure there are clear paths to the dance floor and to the bar. Leave the obstacle course to your next mud run.
- Take the number of guests you have and double that number. This is the absolute bare minimum square footage of your dance floor. 300 Guests? At the very least you would want a 600 square foot dance floor.
- The venue may have floor plans with table options that they have used before. Ask if they have pictures of the options or a paper chart that you can see.
- Usher is a fantastic singer, but let's talk about the ushers for your wedding. You should have at least 1 Usher for every 50 guests.
- The easiest way for your guests to find their seats at the reception is to have a seating chart sign that is arranged alphabetically. Quadruple check before printing to make sure there are no misspelled names or missing guests.

Seating Chart - To Do List

- [ ] _____
- [ ] _____
- [ ] _____
- [ ] _____
- [ ] _____
- [ ] _____
- [ ] _____
- [ ] _____
- [ ] _____
- [ ] _____
- [ ] _____
- [ ] _____
- [ ] _____
- [ ] _____
- [ ] _____
- [ ] _____
- [ ] _____
- [ ] _____

My Thoughts

Table 5	Table 4	Table 3	Table 2	Table 1

Table 10	Table 9	Table 8	Table 7	Table 6

Main Table

Table 11	Table 12	Table 13	Table 14	Table 15

Table 16	Table 17	Table 18	Table 19	Table 20	Table 21

Seating Chart Layout

Bachelorette Party

Bachelorette Party

The bachelorette party isn't about all of your single friends, it's about you. When your maid of honor, or whomever is planning the bachelorette party, is consulting with you about it you should let them know your limitations and expectations. Especially if they are single and ready to mingle which will influence their plans unless your vision is laid out clearly. Here's a pro tip: if you are not a big drinker, don't drink big during your bachelorette party. Nobody wants to see you curled up on the bathroom floor at 9PM after the pre-party and before the actual party begins.

What To Ask Yourself

- Who is going to plan it?
- Do I want a chill bachelorette party, a full out party or something in between?
- Who should be invited?
- Who pays for what?
- What does the itinerary look like?
- Is this going to be local or a destination bachelorette party?
- Are we going to combine the bachelorette and bachelor parties?
- Will it be one day, a weekend or a full on vacation?
- Social Media or no Social Media?

Ideas You Haven't Thought About

- A gift for the bride is not mandatory. You could have one group gift or individual gifts if you so choose but really, the party is the gift.
- Casino party
- Sleepover
- Spa Day
- Resorts
- Piano Bars
- Dancing Class
- Picnic
- Baby Goat Yoga
- Speakeasies
- Hot Air Balloons
- Wine Tasting
- Sailing
- Horseback Riding
- Glamping Trip
- Food Tours
- AirBnB With Day Excursions
- Museum/Gallery VIP Tours
- Sporting Events
- Pool Party

Tips & Tricks

- Matching color or theme outfits. Do I even need to say anything else? So fun!!!
- If the party is going to be boozy, transportation should be lined up throughout the entirety of the festivities.
- Traditionally, the bride will not pay and the rest of the party goers will split the bill.
- Although the tradition is your bridesmaids and groomsmen picking up the tab for your epic party, many times this doesn't happen and you end up picking up some or most of the bill. Keep that in mind for your budget.
- Invites should definitely go out to all of the bridesmaids. Outside of that, any other guests should only be invited with the approval of the bride.
- For your itinerary you should think about the pre-party, having a meal together, a chill activity and an activity that the bride normally wouldn't

do. Don't forget the day after brunch for everyone to relive the fun before departing.

- Once everything is set, let the party crew know what the total cost is sans gratuity, taxes & fees and set a deadline for collecting payment.
- A good time for a bachelorette party is in that 1-3 month range from the wedding. This way the bride is not too overwhelmed with wedding planning, decisions and preparation.
- If your groom has sisters, you may want to include them in the festivities.
- Before the party gets started, make sure if the bride is OK or not OK with Social Media posts that her Mom, colleagues and priest will see. Let the rest of the squad know so you are all on the same page.
- Respect for your partner is key here as well. If you are not comfortable with exotic dancers at his party, you should probably skip it for yours. This also goes for the wild ones in the group trying to talk you into "last chance before you're married" activities which could be a recipe for serious conflict with your love.
- Checking in with your sweetheart every once in a while during your bachelorette party is OK, they don't need a play by play and you should be in the moment with your girls!
- Have a backup plan just in case the unimaginable happens. The Maid of Honor missed her flight. Your outdoor activity gets rained out. Two people canceled at the last minute. You never know.
- If you are the bride and your friends have put on this amazing event for you, stop your bestie who has had too much to drink and is thinking about getting behind the wheel. Pay for their Uber.
- Get the groom to be involved in some way. It could be a message to the bride, answers to questions for a game that you are playing or a surprise (but short) appearance.
- This is the perfect time to test those hangover kits you were thinking about getting for the day after the wedding.
- Have fun games ready for downtime. You may have more than anticipated.

Insider Secrets

- Did you know that there are actual bachelorette party planners? If it's too much to plan for you or the person who is doing it, consider this as an option.
- Keep in mind that not all attendees will have the same ability in their

budget as others. Having a conversation with everyone about what they are comfortable with is essential.

- One person should be planning this along with the bride. Usually it is the maid of honor but you might have a super-planner in your group. The main thing to remember is that too many planners will mean never actually getting a plan done.
- Send out around 5 potential dates (that works for the bride) to all of the guests and see which ones work best for most. Have the guests respond with all of the dates that they can attend. One of the dates will have the majority of invitees.
- The bachelorette party is all about the bride. Focus on her likes/dislikes as well as her personality and plan accordingly. Don't let Single Life Laryssa dictate the itinerary because she will want to up the level of partying that she is used to (which is every weekend). That could mean a hospital trip for Calm Karrie.
- To avoid embarrassment, disappointment or being flat out uncomfortable, speak up about what your expectations are.
- Don't overschedule the day(s). Think about the time it takes in between planned activities for getting ready/refreshed, transportation time & simply wrangling up however many people are in your group.
- Bring a tripod for a phone or camera so you can have more professional-like group photos.
- Pace yourselves so that you can enjoy the whole night or the whole weekend. Do you really want to have the worst hangover after the first night and miss out on the art gallery with martinis tour that was set up for early day two?

Bachelorette Party - To Do List

- [ ] _____
- [ ] _____
- [ ] _____
- [ ] _____
- [ ] _____
- [ ] _____
- [ ] _____
- [ ] _____
- [ ] _____
- [ ] _____
- [ ] _____
- [ ] _____
- [ ] _____
- [ ] _____
- [ ] _____
- [ ] _____
- [ ] _____
- [ ] _____
- [ ] _____

My Thoughts

Bachelor Party

Bachelor Party

I know what you are thinking. We all know the supposed tradition. To be honest, professional dancers are not on the top of the list for today's bachelor party if it's even on the list at all. Most guys would prefer to make memories with their friends by either doing something new or something they love. Outside of my own bachelor parties (yes, I had two) one of the most memorable and fun bachelor parties that I went to was a camping and white water rafting trip with the boys. Regardless of what you do, make sure you communicate everything that goes on with your sweetheart. You don't want them finding out by someone else that was there.

What To Ask Yourself

- Who is going to plan it?
- Do I want a chill bachelor party, a full out party or something in between?
- Who should be invited?
- Who pays for what?
- What does the itinerary look like?
- Is this going to be local or a destination bachelor party?
- Are we going to combine the bachelorette and bachelor parties?
- Will it be one day, a weekend or a full on vacation?
- Social Media or no Social Media?

Things You Haven't Thought About

- Whitewater Rafting
- Snowboarding
- Hiking/Camping
- Casino Party
- Distillery Tours
- Craft Beer Tours
- Golfing
- Fishing
- Pool Party
- Restaurant Crawl
- Speakeasies
- Hunting/Shooting
- Personalized Whiskey/Bourbon Tasting
- Skydiving
- Sporting Events
- Paintball War

Tips & Tricks

- Invite the groomsmen and any other close friends/family that he wants. The best man or whomever is planning the party shouldn't invite people on their own.
- To avoid embarrassment, disappointment or being flat out uncomfortable, speak up about what your expectations are.
- Before the party gets started, make sure if the groom is OK or not OK with Social Media posts that his Mom, sisters and priest will see. Let the rest of the gang know so you are all on the same page.
- Although the tradition is your bridesmaids and groomsmen picking up the tab for your epic party, many times this doesn't happen and you end up picking up some or most of the bill. Keep that in mind for your budget.
- Don't drink & drive. Have transportation lined up for all activities. For the groom to be, if your friend seems buzzed, pay for the Lyft as a thank you for the rad party!
- Communicate with your sweetheart on what the rules should be for each of your parties. Make sure you express what you agree on with your planner and be sure they explain the importance of it so the rest of the crew respects it.

- Before the party, communicate with your sweetheart. Check in, but maybe only a few times a day. After the party tell her everything you'd tell your best friend that couldn't make it. You don't want her to find out through a 3rd party.
- Newsflash! Not all guys dig strip clubs or strippers. Don't go just to fulfill some tradition that may have been started for a bunch of single 22 year olds.
- Hazing is a terrible idea. Yeah, you did it in college, but this is not the way.
- Do something awesome, not just the same old same old. Step a bit outside the squad's comfort zone.
- It's always the best idea for the groom to walk away from the bachelor party with no hospital visits, court dates or STDs. Be the best friend that you are supposed to be.
- For your itinerary you should think about the pre-party, having meals together, a chill activity and an activity that the groom normally wouldn't do. Don't forget the day after brunch for you all to relive the fun before departing.
- Once everything is set, let the party crew know what the total cost is sans gratuity, taxes & fees and set a deadline for collecting payment.
- Have a backup plan just in case the unimaginable happens. The Best Man missed his flight. Your outdoor activity gets rained out. Two people canceled at the last minute. You never know.

Insider Secrets

- This party is all about the groom-to-be. More than likely he has been beaten down with wedding planning so it is time to relax and destress. Make sure you take into consideration his style and personality when planning.
- Send out around 5 potential dates (that works for the groom) to all of the guests and see which ones work best for most. Have the guests respond with all of the dates that they can attend. One of the dates will have the majority of invitees.
- Plan the party 1-3 months before the wedding day. Things will be too hectic the month of.
- Keep in mind that not all attendees will have the same ability in their budget as others. Having a conversation with everyone about what they are comfortable with is essential.
- One person should be planning this along with the groom. Usually it is

the best man but you might have a take charge kind of guy in your group. The main thing to remember is that too many planners will mean never actually getting a plan done.

- Pace yourself. I actually had two bachelor parties. One with real close friends that were in the wedding and one with co-workers. The one with friends was the first one and we partied so hard the first night (as if we were still in college) that the next day and night activities were scrapped for more chill recovery time.
- Don't overschedule the day(s). Think about the time it takes in between planned activities for getting ready, transportation time & simply wrangling up however many people are in your group.
- There are professionals that plan bachelor parties. If nobody on your team is good with that sort of stuff, hire one.

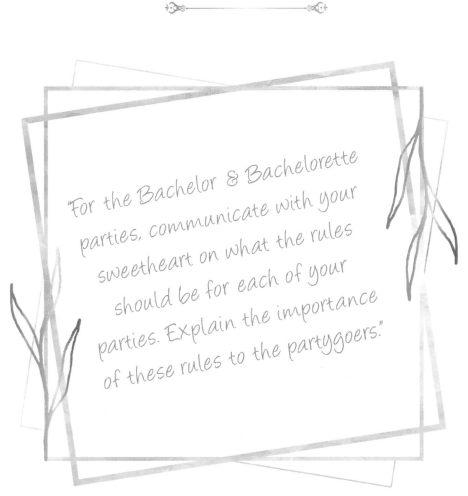

"For the Bachelor & Bachelorette parties, communicate with your sweetheart on what the rules should be for each of your parties. Explain the importance of these rules to the partygoers."

Bachelor Party - To Do List

- [ ] _____
- [ ] _____
- [ ] _____
- [ ] _____
- [ ] _____
- [ ] _____
- [ ] _____
- [ ] _____
- [ ] _____
- [ ] _____
- [ ] _____
- [ ] _____
- [ ] _____
- [ ] _____
- [ ] _____
- [ ] _____
- [ ] _____
- [ ] _____

My Thoughts

Gifts

Gifts

For me, I guess I was kind of lucky to have a cultural tradition of accepting envelopes and not gifts at the wedding. Adam's Italian heritage also had a similar tradition. Watch The Godfather, you'll know what I'm talking about. There were some major benefits to this type of gift receiving. One, you don't have to register at a bunch of places. Two, you can use the cash that you receive in those envelopes to help pay for the wedding or for your honeymoon among other things. If this sounds like something that you'd like to do, it is not as scary to ask as you'd think. Simply let your guests know in your invitation, on your website or in your reminder email that you are accepting this type of gift. You may have some people that give you a traditional wrapped gift but at least you won't get 3 toasters and 5 wine glass sets.

What To Ask Yourself

- ♥ Who are we going to get gifts for?
- ♥ What is the total number of people we are getting gifts for?
- ♥ What are we going to budget per gift?
- ♥ What is our per person budget?
- ♥ Does this per person budget allow us to get the gifts we envisioned?
- ♥ Are we going for inexpensive yet meaningful gifts or gifts that will last a lifetime?
- ♥ Does it make sense and is it thoughtful for the person we are giving it to?
- ♥ Will they be able to use this gift after the wedding day?

Things You Haven't Thought About

- Wedding favors
- Wedding party day-of gifts
- Gifts for your flower girls and/or ring bearers
- The pillow gift
- Welcome baskets for out of town guests
- Thank you gifts for vendors that over delivered (outside of their tip)
- Presents for Parents/Grandparents
- Wedding party proposal gifts

Tips & Tricks

- You may have never heard of a pillow gift like most guys (and many women). This is a special gift that you give your sweetheart that will be waiting for them on their pillow at the end of this very special night. The pillow gift puts the evening over the top with a special sentiment. Highly recommended for the engagement night too!

- Some of the best gifts are functional. I have to tell you that the very best groomsmen gift I ever received (sorry everyone else) was from one of my best friends. It was a small multi-tool. Probably one of the more inexpensive ones this particular brand carried. But this thing has been in my pocket, every day, from day one. I even used it to help change a tire once! Long story.

- Welcome gifts for out of town guests that are spending a lot of money to attend your wedding is a nice touch but not mandatory. They can be simple or elaborate but should have a personal touch. A basket with nice soaps, some beverages and cards with lists of things to do in your city is just one example.

- Some ideas for the ladies in the wedding are: customized memory box, clutches, bracelets, pearl jewelry, personalized wine bottles, custom drawn portraits, etc.

- Some ideas for the gents in the wedding are: flasks, personalized bourbon bottles, personalized coffee tumblers or alcohol tumblers, customized travel bags, multi-tools, minibar travel cases, etc.

- Some ideas for the parents and/or grandparents are: pocket watches, engraved clocks, personalized picture frames, canvas photos, personalized indoor plant pottery, etc.

- When you ask your bridesmaids or groomsmen to be part of your wedding party, some do it in style with a gift. Think about giving a gift that can also be used for the bachelorette/bachelor party or the wedding day like matching outfits, socks, t-shirts, robes or cufflinks.

- Other gift ideas: Sunglasses for kids in the wedding party, custom blankets for kids or throw blankets for adults, leather passport holders, personalized beverage tub, engraved cutting boards or charcuterie boards, cozy slippers, coffee mugs, make-up bags, grill kits, wine openers, etc.
- You may have a close friend or relative assisting you with your wedding. Maybe they are the caterer or the photographer. Outside of the gratuity, you can also let them know how crucial they were to your special day by giving an extra gift at the end of the night.
- For wedding favors, think twice about large gifts or gifts that can spoil/ wilt easily. No, your Mom's best friend isn't going to take home the 2 foot vase with chrysanthemums & wedding color rocks in it.
- Any gift you give should be meaningful. Your monogram and/or wedding date is yours, not the people who are receiving the gift.
- If you are giving tasty gifts in the form of food, sweets or beverages, maybe even scented gifts . . . it is best to try them out first.
- You can DIY party favors but make sure you have the time to complete them. A hybrid DIY would be to purchase ready-made items and then customize them yourselves.

Insider Secrets

- Your maid of honor and best man will typically get a more lavish gift.
- Stay away from bridal party gifts that have to do with the wedding, like your wedding video or wedding pictures. They will be there right with you and likely won't watch it or look at it except every great once in a while.
- Something edible will more than likely be taken home by your guests than a party favor whether it is DIY or purchased.
- A survey for wedding party gifts showed that men preferred alcohol related gifts while women preferred jewelry & beauty items.
- A rule of thumb for any gift is: "Is this something I would want?"
- For wedding favor gifts, think about the season and what could be a fun gift to give your guests.
- Want to relive the night with all of your favorite local guests without actually reliving the night? Think about a ticket to a local sporting event, rent out a movie theater or get tickets to a play, event or park. It can be 6 months after your wedding date and you could have an rsvp ticket as the

wedding favor. Not everyone will attend which means you aren't having to buy everyone a favor. You'd be surprised to find out that this could actually cost you less than getting everyone a personalized gift, half of which will be left behind.

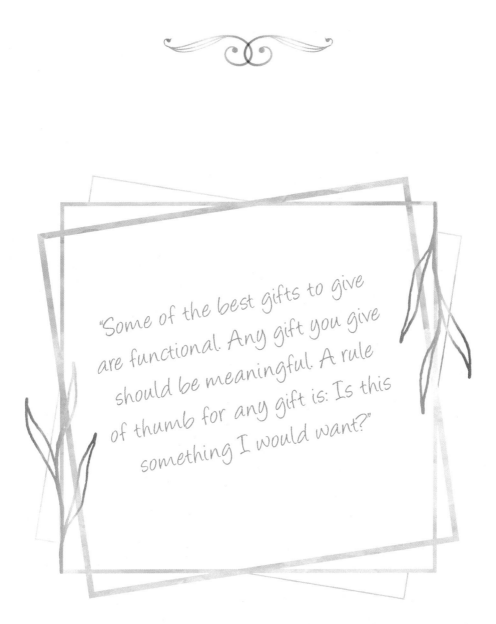

"Some of the best gifts to give are functional. Any gift you give should be meaningful. A rule of thumb for any gift is: Is this something I would want?"

Gifts - To Do List

- [ ] _____
- [ ] _____
- [ ] _____
- [ ] _____
- [ ] _____
- [ ] _____
- [ ] _____
- [ ] _____
- [ ] _____
- [ ] _____
- [ ] _____
- [ ] _____
- [ ] _____
- [ ] _____
- [ ] _____
- [ ] _____
- [ ] _____
- [ ] _____
- [ ] _____

My Thoughts

Business	Contact Name	Phone	Email	Number Of Gifts	Cost Per Gift	Description	Total Estimated Cost	Notes

Notes

Guest(s)	Description Of Gift Received	Thank You Note Sent

Guest(s)	Description Of Gift Received	Thank You Note Sent

Guest(s)	Description Of Gift Received	Thank You Note Sent

Guest(s)	Description Of Gift Received	Thank You Note Sent

Guest(s)	Description Of Gift Received	Thank You Note Sent

Other Things You Might Not Have thought About

Other Things You Might Not Have Thought About

There is so much to do, prepare for and make decisions on that it is difficult to include it all in one wedding planner. You'd be surprised how many no-brainer "of course we are doing that" type of decisions fall by the wayside and become last second thoughts or throw-ins for the wedding. We didn't prepare a thank you speech because it slipped our minds until the day before the wedding. Good thing Adam is quick on his feet and has experience in radio where he had to do live updates and news all the time. If you come across something you hadn't thought about before, make sure you put it in your to-do list or in your wedding planner right away with a checkbox by it. "I'll remember it" usually ends up in "how did I forget about that?" A life hack I like to use if I am out and about and don't have my wedding planner with me is to text myself the thought.

Things You Haven't Thought About

- Writing your thank you speech for the reception
- Wedding couple transportation fees
- Wedding party transportation fees
- Gratuity for drivers
- Shuttle service from hotels that your guests are staying in
- Valet parking service

- Chair covers
- Marriage license fees & bringing the license to the wedding
- Is it outside? Portable heaters might be a hidden cost!
- Asking bridesmaids to be in your wedding in a special way
- Couples massage to relieve stress in the midst of planning
- Hotel rooms the night before the wedding for bridesmaids and groomsmen
- Forgotten items that require a quick trip to be purchased
- An extra blank invitation suite for your photographer to take photos of
- Phone chargers
- Bar decor
- Speaking of the bar. Ice, Ice baby!! You need plenty of it.
- Still speaking of the bar . . . hangover kits are glorious and great gifts for the bridal party too.
- Wedding Insurance. Yes, it's a thing.

Tips & Tricks

- Get a high-end Uber to transport you and your sweetheart after the ceremony and/or reception instead of a limo.
- When thinking of transportation, never fill the vehicle to capacity (whether it is a car, limo, shuttle or bus). Keep things comfortable.
- If you have a shuttle, designate a shuttle pick-up point and start the return shuttle earlier than the very end of the night. We suggest two hours prior to the last song for those guests that don't party hard.
- Get nice pens for the things you and your guests will be signing. Unless a bic ballpoint instead of a Conway Stewart Westminster Teal pen is where you want to save money.
- In the hustle and bustle of planning your wedding, some couples forget to check the validity, update or get a new passport. Don't do that, otherwise your Amalfi Coast honeymoon may turn into an Emerald Coast honeymoon!
- One thing that will WOW your guests is a memorable entranceway. Ask your vendor what types of memorable entrances they have seen created there and if they have pictures.
- Heaters for cold evenings and fans for hot days will save you and your guests.
- Don't forget to have extra cash and your IDs with you on the big day.
- If you are doing a ton of DIY for the wedding, you will want to assign

a set-up lead and a clean up lead. The set-up lead should have an eye for detail and the demeanor of getting people to pitch in yet sweet enough to make them actually want to do it. The breakdown lead should be one of the least likely to be drunk. Maybe relatives or friends who know how to manage people or recruit other not-too-tipsy guests to help out.

Insider Secrets

- Keep about 5% of your budget aside for the cost of random things that you did not think about as long as you are good at sticking to budgets and paying attention to detail. If not, keep 10% set aside. Wait. What!?! There is an extra fee to bring in a vendor that isn't on my venue's preferred vendor list?
- Did you know that destination weddings, when all is said and done, can be more expensive than hometown weddings?
- If you are considering a valet service for your special day, begin by requesting a site visit. Reputable valet companies will go to the venue to meet you for their thoughts on how valet would work there. Make sure they are fully insured, give you a proposal with cost and contract in writing and ask how many people will be there to assist your guests.
- Need to keep kids from going nuts during the reception? Hire a sitter to do crafts, games and movies at the venue.
- Some ceremony & wedding venues won't allow you to do rose petals, rice, confetti or sparklers when you leave. You can replace those with bubbles, ribbon wands, oversized (easy to clean up) confetti or something else unique.

Other Things - To Do List

- [ ] _____
- [ ] _____
- [ ] _____
- [ ] _____
- [ ] _____
- [ ] _____
- [ ] _____
- [ ] _____
- [ ] _____
- [ ] _____
- [ ] _____
- [ ] _____
- [ ] _____
- [ ] _____
- [ ] _____
- [ ] _____
- [ ] _____
- [ ] _____
- [ ] _____

Other Things - To Do List

- [ ] _____
- [ ] _____
- [ ] _____
- [ ] _____
- [ ] _____
- [ ] _____
- [ ] _____
- [ ] _____
- [ ] _____
- [ ] _____
- [ ] _____
- [ ] _____
- [ ] _____
- [ ] _____
- [ ] _____
- [ ] _____
- [ ] _____
- [ ] _____
- [ ] _____

My Thoughts

Music

Music

So you think you can dance? It doesn't really matter if you can or you can't. What matters is that you have the music to make everyone else have a great time and that includes dancing. One of the sweetest things we have encountered was where the DJ asked groups to join the dance floor by the amount of years they had been married. Each group had a song played from that era. Then when all of the single people joined the floor the party really got going. Don't forget all of the generations that will be attending and the music they like when coming up with your playlist.

What To Ask Yourself

- ♥ Are our music preferences different? Does he like the current top 50 while I like the 80s?
- ♥ What can we do to mix our favorite songs if our favorite songs aren't the same?
- ♥ What song do we want to enter the reception to?
- ♥ Do we want to pair up the wedding party now and choose the songs for them or let them agree on a song?
- ♥ Are there certain genres of music that we absolutely do not want played? Sorry Polka & Nu-Metal.
- ♥ Do we want guests to be able to make requests?
- ♥ What are each of our top 10 must have songs?
- ♥ What are each of our top 10 do-not-play songs?

Things You Haven't Thought About

- Getting ready music
- Father-Daughter dance
- Mother-Son dance
- Cake cutting song
- Garter/Bouquet toss songs
- Send-Off song
- Do-Not-Play list
- Cocktail hour music vs reception music
- Microphones for wedding ceremony & toasts
- Sound system
- Karaoke?

Tips & Tricks

- Each of you should choose your top 3 first dance songs, have them ready to play and then reveal your top three back and forth. One of them may be the same, some may be no-go songs and one will come out the clear winner.
- Looking to be super frugal here? Create your own playlist and keep someone you know in charge of pausing and playing it at the right times.
- Want to hire musicians? Check with local high schools, universities & local concert halls for star musicians that aren't used to getting paid for their talent.
- The best DJs can provide music and a sound system as well as lighting. They can play music for cocktail hour, set up sound for any musicians you bring in & provide ambiance by way of lighting throughout the venue if needed or wanted. Ultimately they will be engaging and get your guests involved. You want the DJ that sees certain music isn't getting the dance floor full and can switch it up without you even noticing.
- You most definitely want to have a "Don't Play" list. Imagine having a great time and then a song you both hate comes on. Seriously, why did they just play the Baby Shark remix!?!
- You probably won't believe this, but some couples actually forget to have a designated dance floor among the tables for the reception. Make sure one is designated and that it makes sense.
- If your reception is going to be lit until Midnight, you may not want to start the dance party at 6PM. Your Coachella friends might be up for 6

hours of dancing, but almost everyone else will call it a night way before then.

♥ Ask if clean versions will be played. Even if clean versions are played, does Great Grandma Georgia really need to hear "Ain't No Fun" by Snoop Dogg?

♥ Your ceremony will typically have classical or acoustic music. Your Cocktail hour & dinner should be more upbeat and hit multiple generations from the 20's like big band to the 60's like the Beatles to the 80's like Pet Shop Boys (Lucy's favorite). The reception should get people dancing but also keep in mind your guests. Dance music means different things to different age groups.

Insider Secrets

♥ Avoid a super long first dance song. If you don't like people watching you closely in normal everyday life, you definitely won't want to have all eyes on you during a 6 minute romantic version of Rick Astley's "Never Gonna' Give You Up" for your first dance. 3 Minutes is the sweet spot.

♥ Feel free to give your DJ or Band a long list of songs you like, but don't tell them they should play all of them. They are good at what they do. They will probably play songs they know will get the crowd dancing that will also fit your music style. 50 songs is about 3 hours of music. Don't hand them 100 songs on a list, keep it around 30-40. Highlight the must play songs and don't micromanage.

♥ Some ceremony locations may not let you choose whatever songs you want played. Check with the location and officiant if there are any limitations.

♥ Raid your playlists and create a combined list to play when you are getting ready & during photo shoots. Bring your bluetooth speakers.

♥ Want everyone on the dance floor? Get all of the guests to take a group photo and then have the DJ or Band play the best song they know will get people dancing right after.

♥ Another great way to get people on the dance floor is to start with a slow song, ask the parents to join and then have couples join by years married (50 years come join, 40 years, 30 years, 20, 10, 5, 1 . . . just met tonight!)

♥ Don't forget to choose a Send-Off song. It's not necessarily the last song of the night, but it will be the song played when your transportation arrives and you leave the venue. A celebratory song that also acts as a cue.

Music - To Do List

- [ ] _____
- [ ] _____
- [ ] _____
- [ ] _____
- [ ] _____
- [ ] _____
- [ ] _____
- [ ] _____
- [ ] _____
- [ ] _____
- [ ] _____
- [ ] _____
- [ ] _____
- [ ] _____
- [ ] _____
- [ ] _____
- [ ] _____
- [ ] _____
- [ ] _____

My Thoughts

Ceremony Music	Cocktail Hour Music	Bridal Party/Parents Entrance Songs	Grand Entrance Song

First Dance	Dinner Must Play Songs	Dancing Must Play Songs	Dancing Must Play Songs
Father/Daughter Dance			
Mother/Son Dance			
Boquet Toss Song			

Coordination

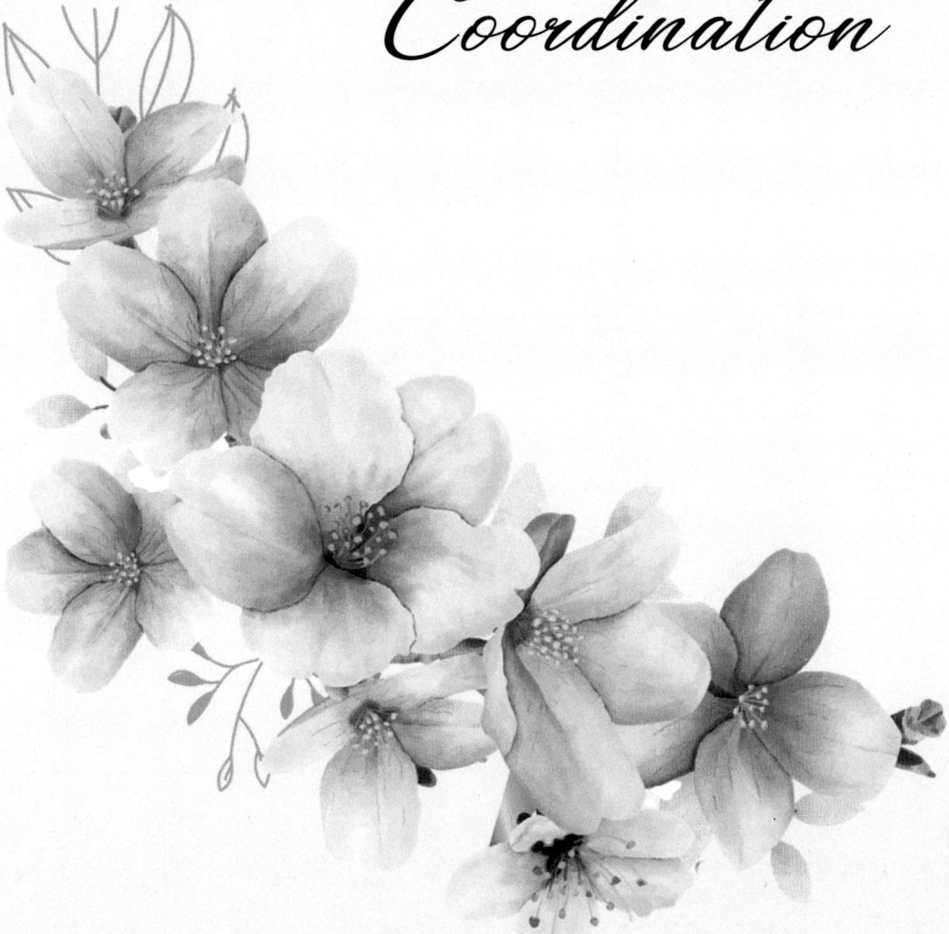

Coordination

Whether you are looking to use this wedding planner as a way to coordinate your wedding, perhaps even the Ultimate Wedding Planner Secret Sheets or through a wedding coordinator, it is imperative that you have someone assigned to help coordinate. The easiest route, of course, is to have a coordinator. For those of you wanting to save some money, we'd suggest using someone from your family or circle of friends to help coordinate. We had a coordinator from the venue where our wedding was that helped the coordination of vendors in and out of the venue but not really coordinating the schedule for the day of. For that, we entrusted Adam's cousin who was a stickler for details and also was very good at coordinating events. When we asked her, a sly smile rose upon her face to which she replied "Oh, I'm good at making sure people know they have to do their job." We knew we could count on her. Thanks Dawn!

What To Ask A Wedding Coordinator

- Are there services not included that I should consider?
- Do you advocate for us if there are issues with vendors?
- For day-of packages do we have access to you prior to the wedding day? How far in advance do you plan?
- Will you have any assistants working with you?
- Do you do walk-throughs of the venue to become familiar and visualize how the day should be coordinated?
- Do you only work with a certain list of vendors or can we select our own?
- What is your communication with the other vendors like leading up to the event?

- Do you organize and distribute key parts of the process such as vendor insurance, timelines, vendor meals, set-up & break-down?
- Do you create day-of timelines and, if so, how far in advance do you do this?
- What is your style when coordinating weddings?
- Could you tell me about how you solved big issues that came up during a previous client's wedding?
- What is the typical number of meetings that we will have throughout the planning process?
- Would you be contacting me weekly, bi weekly or another time interval to discuss coordination?
- Do you provide an emergency bridal kit for day-of and what would be in it if you do?
- What details do you need for the wedding and when would you need it?

Things You Haven't Thought About

- Timeline creation (detailed)
- Wedding vendor master lists
- Designated problem solver
- End of evening preservation (someone to take your things home)

Tips & Tricks

- Wedding Planners help you make decisions that relate to the look and feel of your wedding in order to make your dreams and thoughts a reality. A wedding coordinator is all about making things happen as smoothly as possible. It is all about logistics.
- Create a cut-off date for major changes. After that date you will have made the key decisions and the stress that coincides with them will be lifted off of your shoulders.
- Alphabetize your seating or escort cards in advance. Can you imagine how difficult it is to thumb through the cards the day of or, worse yet, while your guests are arriving.
- Ditch your phones. All day. Everything that you normally check will still be there when the ceremony and reception is over. Assign a contact person (usually a day-of planner/coordinator/friend/family member) for vendors, siblings, wedding party & parents to call if something happens. All of your vendors should know that they are the one to be contacted if

needed. Make sure they are good problem solvers.

- ♥ Leave a special voicemail message or autoresponder text for the day. Let people know you will be unavailable as you marry the man or woman of your dreams and won't be checking any messages.
- ♥ When you assign seating for your guests, think it through carefully. Seat people with those they know. Sit singles together maybe with a fun couple or two. Cousin Jerry & Jessica are 13, maybe they should sit with other kids instead of adults and DEFINITELY not with your college buddies.
- ♥ Let your wedding party give toasts, but let them know in advance that they should keep it to around three minutes or less. The last thing you want is the unprepared bridesmaid rambling on about coloring princess dresses with permanent markers in the 2nd grade. Also, keep the mic away from your best friend Juan, whose life mission has been to embarrass you (or pay you back for your toast).
- ♥ Think about the time of your ceremony and wedding and when the sun sets. This may be a perfect time for pictures instead of the bouquet toss.
- ♥ For DIY weddings, make sure you have designated people to bring things to the venue(s) as well as people to take things home from the venue(s). The last thing you want is the venue to throw away all of the hard work you put into the wedding decor (and plan to re-use).
- ♥ Create an email account strictly for your wedding. You are going to get A LOT of emails and "offers".
- ♥ Don't forget about your honeymoon preparations before your special day especially if you are leaving shortly after the wedding. Make a list, check it twice, don't forget the things that are naughty and nice.
- ♥ Designate someone to gather photo groups & VIPs for your formal portraits. You don't want to be running around trying to find your niece who is gravitating towards the charcuterie instead of capturing the moment with you.
- ♥ Make a plan for guests who may want to party after the reception is over.
- ♥ You may reach a point where you are tired of making decisions. This is where the wedding coordinator or even wedding planners come into play. You definitely do not want to be making last minute decisions on your wedding day. They'll make the right decisions for you based on your thorough conversations.
- ♥ Let's talk about the timeline. Make sure your timeline includes arrival times of every vendor as well as needed set-up times. Add a little bit extra to the times they quoted.
- ♥ Ask your coordinator before you book them if they will be attending the wedding rehearsal. If the answer is no, move along.

- Taking family & VIP photos before the ceremony could save you from tracking people down and will also relieve stress in between the ceremony and reception when many photographers opt to take these photos.
- Don't forget about choosing the right best man. This person should make sure all of the groomsmen have everything they need to dress for the wedding (and return them on time if rented). He should have a groom's emergency kit, make sure things run on schedule with little stress, hold onto the wedding rings, make sure the groom eats and drinks and might even be the witness for the marriage license.

Insider Secrets

- Tell Your bridal party to be there 30 minutes before you actually need them there.
- Walk through the day with coordination in mind. You can do this in your head but you'll definitely want to do it at least once in person as well. How and where are your guests going to sign your guestbook? Does it make sense? When do they get their programs and by who? Think about this day from your guest's perspective.
- Is there a significant amount of time between the ceremony and the reception? Add some suggestions to your program of what to do in between for out of town guests.
- Have you thought about a completely separate reception dress? Who doesn't like a wardrobe change mid-performance?
- The larger the wedding party the longer it takes to do just about everything. Imagine having to get 8 bridesmaids and 8 groomsmen all together to do one thing. Multiple times throughout the day.
- Day-of wedding coordination should actually include the month of your wedding.
- Not all day-of coordinators include the same amount of support? It is very important to be clear on what is included and see if it fits your needs.
- Do you have young children? Think about hiring a babysitter for the wedding day to take care of them while you enjoy your moment.
- Have a tracking system in place for vendors, RSVPs, etc. We know of a really good one . . . it's our Ultimate Wedding Planner Sheets that you can keep in the cloud through your google or excel accounts and share with whomever you want. Most of the sheets are printed in this book, but if you want a digital copy that calculates things for you and that you can share, it is the perfect companion. You can get it at https://www.infinancer.com/weddings

if you already haven't done so.

- 💜 Designate one of your Maid Of Honors to fix your dress and vail when necessary.
- 💜 Designate someone to load gifts and cards into a specific vehicle. Preferably someone that doesn't get too toasty during parties.
- 💜 Day-Of coordinators from your preferred venue may not be working for you as much as they are working for the venue. Keep this in mind.
- 💜 If your wedding coordinator has assistants for the wedding, they should be doing all the walk-throughs with the coordinator.

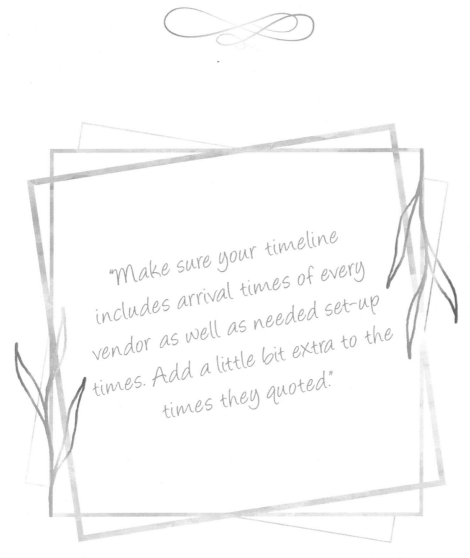

"Make sure your timeline includes arrival times of every vendor as well as needed set-up times. Add a little bit extra to the times they quoted."

Coordination - To Do List

- [ ] _____
- [ ] _____
- [ ] _____
- [ ] _____
- [ ] _____
- [ ] _____
- [ ] _____
- [ ] _____
- [ ] _____
- [ ] _____
- [ ] _____
- [ ] _____
- [ ] _____
- [ ] _____
- [ ] _____
- [ ] _____
- [ ] _____
- [ ] _____
- [ ] _____

Coordination - To Do List

- [ ] _____
- [ ] _____
- [ ] _____
- [ ] _____
- [ ] _____
- [ ] _____
- [ ] _____
- [ ] _____
- [ ] _____
- [ ] _____
- [ ] _____
- [ ] _____
- [ ] _____
- [ ] _____
- [ ] _____
- [ ] _____
- [ ] _____
- [ ] _____
- [ ] _____

My Thoughts

Coordinator Or Planner	Contact Name	Phone	Email	Number Of Hours	Day Of Or Full Service	Number Of Contacts Before Day-Of	Total Estimated Cost	Notes

Notes

Detailed Wedding Day Timeline

Detailed Wedding Day Timeline

Lucy & I needed a detailed wedding day timeline and the ones that I was finding online just weren't cutting it for us. Ultimately, I decided to create our own. It has been used by friends, family and clients ever since and is in our Ultimate Wedding Planner Secret Sheets which is a great companion to this book. What a detailed wedding day timeline does for you is let you see what will unfold throughout your special day and it will guide the person you have in charge of coordinating the day. Very much a key part of your wedding day planning!

What To Ask Yourselves

- 💜 What does setup include?
- 💜 How much buffer do we want to include between each major timeline event?
- 💜 Are we getting ready at a different location other than where the ceremony takes place?
- 💜 How much time do we need for hair and makeup? Are the bridesmaids, moms and grandmas also getting their hair and makeup done as well?
- 💜 Is the ceremony at a different location than the reception?
- 💜 How long does it take to get between locations?
- 💜 Are you doing photos pre-ceremony or post ceremony?
- 💜 Are we doing a first look?

- How long will the ceremony take?
- How long will the cocktail hour take?
- Will you be greeting each guest as they arrive at the reception site?
- When should we serve the food (before you and your guests get hangry)?
- What dances are you doing at the reception (bridal party entrance, father/daughter, mother/son, first dance, etc.)?
- How long will the cake cutting be?
- Will there be wardrobe changes?
- What other scheduled activities are you including (garter toss, bouquet toss, group photo, etc,)?
- How many toasts will there be?
- Will there be a last dance?
- Will there be a scheduled grand exit?
- When is the cutoff time for music?
- When does the breakdown begin?

Things You Haven't Thought About

- Transportation time between locations
- All the different dances/entrances you might have scheduled
- Wardrobe changes
- Talking to each guest during the receiving line
- Breakfast & lunch plans before the reception
- Sunset/Golden hour photos
- First look at ceremony site & first photos as a married couple at the reception site before guests arrive
- First look for parents
- Alone time between ceremony & reception
- Letter/gift exchange between the couple (and the fact that happy tears might mess up makeup)

Tips & Tricks

- Timing is everything! Include a buffer for each timeline event and you will not be running around like crazy to catch up, or worse yet, cutting some things you had planned out of the timeline.
- Transportation time must be included. Use our BFF, Google, to find out typical travel times between all locations and add about 10 minutes to it. Google Maps will allow you to check specific times of the day and will

have an average commute time. Making sure there are no special events that can affect travel time is a must as well.

- 💜 Don't forget to place cultural traditions into the timeline.
- 💜 If you host an afterparty (post-reception), make sure that this as well as the time to travel to that location is part of your timeline.
- 💜 Signing of your wedding license should be included.
- 💜 Are you planning on toasts by the fathers? Make it a welcome toast early on in the reception.
- 💜 If you are religious and plan to have a blessing of the meal, you should add that to your timeline.
- 💜 Coordinate with all of your vendors on your timeline. Let them see it well in advance so that they can suggest or tell you what changes need to be made. You may need to do this a few times before all vendors sign off on the timeframe for their particular responsibility.
- 💜 Don't let cocktail hour go for over an hour. You really want cocktail hour to be a buffer time for people to arrive and for you to check off some things on your timeline like photos or alone time. It also gives your guests some time to mingle before they are seated.
- 💜 Having your timeline of events pushed back even just a few times doesn't seem like a big deal until your overtime charges come in from your vendors.
- 💜 There is such a thing as a first look for parents and close friends/relatives outside of your bridal party. If this is something you want your photographer to capture, make sure it is in your timeline and on their "must have" list. The participants should know about it too so it doesn't take 15 minutes to find grandpa.
- 💜 If you are using shuttles to and from hotels or from the ceremony to the reception site, make sure you have specific times (usually multiple times) that the shuttles will be leaving and picking up guests. Place them on your invites and/or wedding website as well as on your timeline.

Insider Secrets

- 💜 Start with your ceremony time and work your way backwards when creating your timeline. After you get to the beginning of the day you can then start working on the timeline from the ceremony on.
- 💜 Find out when sunset is. You do not want to miss an opportunity for golden hour photos if your wedding is in that timeframe.
- 💜 Many couples forget to place their formal Thank You speech into the

timeline and that means it is usually forgotten.

♥ Toast speeches! Say no to an open mic during this time. Let the DJ or MC of the wedding know who will be giving toasts. We went to a wedding once and it felt like the toasts went on for about an hour because it was open to anyone. Yes, the 2nd cousin 3 times removed on your stepmom's side who had a few too many will jump on the mic and talk about the one (and only time) she met you.

♥ Adam & I had his best friend and my cousin perform a song at the wedding. This took place near the beginning of the reception right after we sat at our table. We almost forgot to add it to the timeline but luckily caught it. This would have been an obvious oversight if we didn't catch it. Just think about it, the DJ wouldn't have known to announce it. They would have been sitting there until our day-of coordinator figured out what needed to happen. Double and triple check your timeline. Have others heavily involved in the wedding do so as well.

♥ Add an hour to hair and makeup on your timeline. This happens to be the number one reason timelines are destroyed on a wedding day.

♥ After your timeline is triple-checked and set, the moment your wedding day begins is the moment you forget about the timeline. This should be in someone else's hands. Yes, you will have an idea of what is happening next and may even know if you are ahead or behind, but don't worry about it. Enjoy your day!!!

Timeline - To Do List

- [ ] _____
- [ ] _____
- [ ] _____
- [ ] _____
- [ ] _____
- [ ] _____
- [ ] _____
- [ ] _____
- [ ] _____
- [ ] _____
- [ ] _____
- [ ] _____
- [ ] _____
- [ ] _____
- [ ] _____
- [ ] _____
- [ ] _____
- [ ] _____

My Thoughts

Activity	Time								
1. Pre-Wedding Activities									
1a. Pre-Wedding Activity: Ladies									
1b. Pre-Wedding Activity: Guys									
1c. Pre-Wedding Activity: Vendor/Event Set-up/Shuttle									

Activity	Time									
1c. Pre-Wedding Activity: Vendor/Event Set-Up/Shuttle (Continued)										
2. Ceremony										
3. Cocktail Hour/Photos										

Activity	Time								
4. Reception									
5. Breakdown & Clean-Up									

Destination Wedding

Destination Wedding

Who hasn't thought about a destination wedding? Less to worry about. You can invite people knowing that most won't make the trip. The destination can double as your honeymoon. So many things that make your wedding less stressful. There happens to be a caveat though. One of our friends had a destination wedding and the long distance coordination seemed to stress them out just as much, especially considering the language barriers they faced. They also felt that their honeymoon wasn't really a honeymoon because they had family & friends there having a vacation too and many wanted to spend time with them after the wedding. Not a lot of days full of alone time to celebrate their new status as a married couple and explore the area together without someone wanting to join in or have the same excursion planned.

What To Ask The Destination Contact

- Are there any other events taking place that week?
- Do you have experience hosting weddings with the number of guests I anticipate having?
- What is the weather like during the time of our arrival?
- Are there packages or is everything booked individually?
- How customizable is the wedding?
- Do you price your weddings per guest, for the desired space or some other form of calculation?
- Do you offer different spaces for the ceremony as well as the reception or is it all done in the same location?
- Could you tell me about the different spaces you have for weddings?

- Do you create the seating charts and cards or do we have to bring our own?
- What sets you apart from other resorts in the area? I am considering these

_____

_____

- Is the resort child friendly or is it adult only even for weddings?
- Is a wedding rehearsal dinner included in the packages?
- Do you have an on-site coordinator and will they be available to us before our arrival as well as the day-of?
- Do you offer group discounts?
- Do you combine wedding and honeymoon packages or do they have to be booked individually?
- Do you have shuttle service to and from the airport and local attractions?
- What type of amenities do you have on site?
- Do you have makeup artists and hair stylists available for the wedding party?
- Do you have in-house photographers and can we see their work?
- Do you have a wide range of food to choose from to create a menu?
- Do you have recommendations for any vendors that you do not have in-house?
- Is there a dress code for guests?
- What types of flowers are ordered for the wedding?
- What are the contingency plans for unforeseen circumstances that may affect the ceremony or reception?
- What is the deposit, when is it due and when is the balance due?
- Are there any legal formalities that we should know about or have to complete before or upon our arrival?
- What documents do you need in order to hold a wedding at your venue?

Things You Haven't Thought About

- You will not be in control of the planning and vendors at a destination wedding like you are in a traditional wedding.
- How disappointed will you be if certain people can't make it?
- Will family and friends be upset that you are having a destination wedding and may not be able to attend?
- Different countries may require additional documentation or completion of additional paperwork to be married, even at a resort.

- Are you planning on continuing your honeymoon there or will you be traveling elsewhere for the honeymoon?
- Will you include excursions for guests to enjoy with you?
- If you have pets, who will watch them?
- Transport of the wedding dress/suit/tuxedo and steaming after arrival.

Tips & Tricks

- Most of your invited guests will be unable to attend. This might even include potential bridesmaids & groomsmen.
- It's probably important to find out if it is legal to be married in the country you are considering. You may even be required to take a blood test in some countries.
- Consider what you are wearing at your destination wedding. If you are in a Bohemian A-Line Chiffon Long Sleeve Wedding Dress and your sweetheart has a 3 piece tuxedo with a tail for your late August Cozumel wedding on the beach when it is humid and 95 degrees... you may want to place a bet on who will pass out first.
- If you are continuing your honeymoon at the same place as the destination wedding, be ready to run into your guests throughout your "getaway".
- You may be uncomfortable with hiring a photographer you have never met and can't communicate with until your arrival. Balance the cost of hiring a photographer there or flying a photographer out with you. It might even cost you less than if they were doing the wedding in your backyard.
- If you are friends with Steve Aoki you may want to fly him out to DJ your wedding.
- Your wedding website will be slightly different when having a destination wedding. You should be including transportation information, nearby attractions, excursions and details of the resort if applicable. Think Rick Steves here.
- Give your guests different accommodation options just as you would for a local wedding.
- Welcome gifts are a fantastic way to thank all of the guests that traveled to attend your wedding. If it is a beachy wedding, think of beachy gifts. Are you having a wedding in Monterosso Al Mare? Think Italian inspired gifts.
- If possible, check out the wedding destination in person in advance.
- Ship decor or other items (not your wedding day attire) ahead of time.

Don't be surprised if it is lost in transit however. Have a back-up plan.

- Plan some optional and fun activities with your guests. They are having a mini vacation as well as attending your wedding.
- Ask for a room block and all of the details and requirements to secure one.
- Language barriers may present unique problems when getting things planned and done. Take this into consideration or start your DuoLingo courses right now.
- See if the destination will comp a one year anniversary suite if you complete your hotel block.

Insider Secrets

- Set your budget first and then find ways to stay within the budget. Because you have less control over costs, it is best to get an after fees and extra charges pricing for packages as well as seeing if certain things can be customized for reduced pricing.
- Hire a local wedding planner if one is not included in your package.
- Destination wedding details need earlier attention than traditional weddings. You should be sending save-the-dates at least 12 months in advance and invitations 6 months in advance for guests to schedule, plan and book the trip.
- If choosing a beach wedding, it is important to know how much of a buffer there will be between invited guests and the fraternity brothers from Rhode Island who are doing shots in speedos while chanting expletives at the "lightweight" in their group.
- You may need to select from a list of preferred vendors that the destination provides or you may have to research vendors yourself. Be prepared if the closest thing you can get to meeting them ahead of time is a Zoom call.
- Make sure your absolute must-have guests can attend before sending out all of your invitations. You may decide to scrap the idea of a destination wedding if most of the key people you want there can't make it.
- Ask for a virtual walk through of all of the most important aspects of the wedding before deciding on a venue or resort.

Destination Wedding - To Do List

- [ ] _____
- [ ] _____
- [ ] _____
- [ ] _____
- [ ] _____
- [ ] _____
- [ ] _____
- [ ] _____
- [ ] _____
- [ ] _____
- [ ] _____
- [ ] _____
- [ ] _____
- [ ] _____
- [ ] _____
- [ ] _____
- [ ] _____
- [ ] _____

Destination Wedding - To Do List

- [ ] _____
- [ ] _____
- [ ] _____
- [ ] _____
- [ ] _____
- [ ] _____
- [ ] _____
- [ ] _____
- [ ] _____
- [ ] _____
- [ ] _____
- [ ] _____
- [ ] _____
- [ ] _____
- [ ] _____
- [ ] _____
- [ ] _____
- [ ] _____

Destination Wedding - To Do List

- [ ] _____
- [ ] _____
- [ ] _____
- [ ] _____
- [ ] _____
- [ ] _____
- [ ] _____
- [ ] _____
- [ ] _____
- [ ] _____
- [ ] _____
- [ ] _____
- [ ] _____
- [ ] _____
- [ ] _____
- [ ] _____
- [ ] _____
- [ ] _____

My Thoughts

Conclusion

Conclusion

Weddings are not fairy tales. Nothing is ever perfect. However, this is where you begin writing a story of the both of you as a couple. Ultimately what we want to impress upon you is to enjoy the process of planning, be in the moment and we especially want you to bask in the glory of your love. Also, don't sweat the small stuff on the day of your wedding. If the people you put in charge are good and have been directed to handle issues on their own, you won't know what went wrong and they'll get it corrected on your behalf.

We hope that First Yes, Then I Do has made you laugh, made you think, revealed some things to you that you haven't thought about and given you some tips and tricks that will help you. We also hope that what you have read will save you money, time and stress along the way. Remember to make a commitment to your budget and start your marriage on the right foot with as little debt as possible and as many smiles as your faces can handle on your special first day as a married couple.

Share The Love

If you loved this book and found that even the smallest tip has helped you in your planning or elevated your wedding, please reach out to us at firstyesthenido@infinancer.com with your story.

As mentioned in the beginning and throughout this book, we offer many other services, coaching, bootcamps & courses that you may find helpful or that you may want to encourage a friend to take advantage of. Here is a list of some of those:

The Ultimate Wedding Planner Spreadsheets

A single spreadsheet with 27 tabs that cover each of the major areas discussed in First Yes, Then I Do! It's a digital planner that you can fill out and share with your sweetheart as well as anyone involved in the wedding as you add to it. Budget calculators, guest lists, seating charts, full year planner, a wedding day schedule and a detailed wedding day timeline just to name a few tabs that will help keep you from pulling your hair out (or sharing the personal notes you wrote down in this book). You can find this at http://www.infinancer.com/weddings

The FREE Ultimate Proposal Guide

We know YOU are getting married, but if you want to help someone that is about to get engaged then give them this link to get some crucial tips that will help them find the right ring and propose the right way. You can send them to this totally free guide at https://www.infinancer.com/proposals

Metals, Diamonds & How To Recognize Quality In Jewelry

A video tutorial on the different types of metals, metal education, upkeep education, diamond education as well as how to recognize generational quality when shopping for jewelry. This is also one of the key components of Legacy & Leverage: How To Get Engaged The Right Way & Buy With Confidence (also perfect for your friends who are about to propose). You can find this at https://www.infinancer.com/jewelry

Pre-Marriage Financial Bootcamp

This life-changing coaching session can be done either through one-on-one coaching or group coaching. In the session, some of the topics covered include individual finances, communication with your sweetheart about financial topics, teamwork when married, creating a plan towards financial freedom, legacy building and much more. Opening communication on this topic saves marriages!

You can find this at https://www.infinancer.com/bootcamp

I Love Lucy Lashes

If you want to learn more about eyelash extensions, lash lifts or if you'd like to book an appointment to get some flirty lashes for your wedding, a special event or "just because", you can do just that with Lucy at https://www.ilovelucylashes.com

Powerful & Meaningful Personal, Financial or Business Coaching

Have you always wanted to ditch old, bad habits and replace them with new and life enhancing habits? Do you need accountability to get you started and keep pushing you to reach the goals and levels in life you deserve? Perhaps you are starting a business or are thinking of starting a business and need some guidance. If you are interested in changing your trajectory in life, whether it is through personal coaching, financial coaching or business coaching, you can book a Discovery Session with Adam at https://www.infinancer.com

The Legacy Story Podcast

Many people are rushing through life without focusing on the areas that will create their legacy. Your Legacy Story can come in many different forms, but are you missing the one that will result in true generational change? This podcast explores Adam's own journey, his topics in coaching & the stories of others in a way that will inspire you to take action and create your next Legacy Story. Find it everywhere you listen to podcasts like Spotify, Apple, Google, Amazon, Tune-In, iHeart & more or go to the website below for a direct link to your favorite way to listen to the podcast https://www.infinancer.com/podcast

About the Authors

Adam Solomine

Adam Solomine spent 20 years in the engagement, wedding and diamond jewelry industry and has had conversations with thousands of couples and hundreds of vendors. Soon after, he shifted his focus to helping others overcome their fears of changing their life and creating a legacy through habits, mindset and accountability. Adam prides himself on the impactful and meaningful coaching he provides and enjoys hearing from his clients on how he has changed their trajectory in life. Aside from coaching, Adam loves spending time with his wife and three little girls (even though he is outnumbered). Keep an eye out for new coaching offerings, books and new episodes of his podcast "Legacy Story". Be sure to follow him @InFinancer.

Lucy Solomine

Lucy Solomine met her husband while working in the engagement and wedding jewelry industry but her true passion was in beauty. After getting married, she went after her dreams and attended Paul Mitchell the School for cosmetology where she performed at the top of her class. She focused on hair during her studies and became a hairstylist right after graduation. Lucy was a hairstylist for a few years when a talented lash artist, who also happened to be her Aunt, encouraged her to train under her to learn lashes. That's exactly what she did! Her peers & clients consistently noted her attention to detail as well as how long their lash retention was and she soon was recognized as a Master Lash Artist. If Lucy is not in the Dallas area, you can usually find her with her husband and three daughters on a beach somewhere. Follow her on social media @ilovelucylashes.

My Thoughts

My Thoughts

My Thoughts

My Thoughts

My Thoughts

My Thoughts